*What everyone should
know about*

Leadership
and
Church Structure

*In the pulpit
and out*

Dennis D. Moses

*What everyone should
know about*

Leadership
and
Church Structure

*In the pulpit
and out*

Dennis D. Moses

Asterisk * denotes author's personal experiences.

PUBLISHED BY:
BRENTWOOD CHRISTIAN PRESS
4000 BEALLWOOD AVENUE
COLUMBUS, GEORGIA 31904

...may every Elisha have an Elijah to help them find the mantle of their calling, every Joshua a Moses to place honor upon them as they answer, and every Timothy a Paul to mentor them as they go...

Dedication...

To my family, who allowed me to "hole up in the study" all those hours to see this book written.

My wife Cissy. A husband could ask for no better wife, nor children a better mother. You have ministered by my side, encouraged me when I doubted, supported me in my efforts, and most importantly, loved me without compromise. I could not have done it without you.

My children. Cody and Elizabeth. For all the time you gave me, sacrificing to keep the house quiet while I wrote. Thanks for letting me know you would have preferred to have been with me. Your love is strengthening.

Contents

Foreword

It is a great honor and privilege to recommend this reference book of wisdom and knowledge to all, especially to those who are in leadership. I have had the unique pleasure of knowing and sharing with the author, Dennis Moses, many hours of personal fellowship. He and I have spent much time in discussing the merits and need for a book of this type. He has given long and exhaustive hours researching, compiling and writing this text.

I have found Dennis to be a very sincere and concerned individual, who deeply cares about the daily operation of churches. The information contained herein will guide you in developing both physical and spiritual leadership in the area of church administration. If you will adhere to the principles set forth, you will not fall into errors that have entangled part of the Body of Christ through lack of knowledge.

This book will be a great tool in laying a good foundation for the operation of a church, and also in correcting errors of administration in the elder-ship and the governing board of the church. Likewise, it will open the windows to God's blessings for you through the knowledge contained within its covers when these principles are applied to the church/ministry.

Don Krider, Director
World Wide Ministries
Fresno, California

Preface

I argued with God, I really did. When it became obvious that He was directing me to write this material, I stood like Moses at the burning bush voicing reasons why I was not the one. He reminded me that I had been trained my entire ministry for what needed to be said, and that when the book was successful it would be because of Him. I realized that the burden had been placed, and it was not going away, so I asked for His anointing as I took up the pen. He honored that request, covering me as I worked on this book with the same anointing I felt when I preached.

Paul said in Eph. 4:1, "I beseech you that ye walk worthy of the vocation wherewith ye are called." My question is, "How can anyone do so if he is not equipped?" My greatest desire is for leaders to be equipped with tools that will give them everything necessary to be effective in their leadership roles. I want to pass on some of the practical experiences of leadership that I have had in my years of ministry, giving examples that would keep others from having to learn some lessons the way I had to...by "hard knocks." (These experiences are denoted in the book by asterisks *.) I also hope to encourage lay persons to support and work with their leaders.

Through the years the church has been divided over many things. Leadership principles should not be one of them. I have attempted to present a scriptural view of this subject, taking care to not "denominationalize" it. In doing so, I will only define the pieces of church structure, leaving the utilization of these pieces to the leading of the Holy Spirit. An entire chapter will be spent discussing what it means to be a leader -- understanding the call, knowing the commitment, placing leaders into office, launching ministries, developing principles of leadership, recognizing the characteristics of a godly leader. Discussion will include things that can hinder our effectiveness, and explore topics that oftentimes might be skirted -- authority, submission, priorities and relationships. I will define the role of the pastor, look at the ministry of elders, deacons, and other leadership areas in the church. And I will not leave out the congregation, rather discuss their supporting role in seeing the vision of the ministry carried out. Lastly, I will define the "legal" or governmental structure of the corporation, supply some examples and suggestions for how its structure can be properly (and scripturally) implemented.

This book has been written with the support and backing of my pastor and church. The material has been thoroughly scrutinized by godly men. I wrote it with the words of the prophet Habakkuk ringing in my heart, "Write the vision, and make it plain upon tables, that he may run that readeth it". Now I submit it with this prayer on my lips, "God, anoint it to the reader's heart as fervently as you did the writer."

Dennis D. Moses

About the Author ...

After listening to a message by Billy Graham, Dennis, at the age of 12, walked into his bedroom and invited Christ into his heart. It was not long before he knew that God had called him to minister and answered that call, preaching his first message at the age of 16. From that beginning he has been busy preaching, teaching, and working in other leadership ministries.

Contrary to expectations the Lord led him to attend a secular college instead of a seminary. His major in mathematics opened the door for a career working with two consecutive companies in his home town. First as a computer programmer/analyst and more recently as an applications development specialist, he has worked the last 15 years leading projects in a variety of areas. This project-lead capacity has taught him how to supervise and organize both people and project tasks to their maximum benefit, honing people skills that have been beneficial in his ministry as well.

His ministry has been as unusual as was his turn toward secular work, and as full-time. For God had prepared the way for him to be able to support himself financially and at the same time work in an associate position in a church that could not afford additional staff. There he worked side by side through the tenure of two pastors until he was led to move to a church in his home town in 1990, where since that time, Dennis has served as co-pastor and as associate pastor. His ministry in these churches allowed the senior pastors the ability to be away from the church as needed, and Dennis built a rapport with other pastors in the area that allowed him to fill their pulpits so they could do the same.

But there was more. For several years in the beginning of his ministry Dennis taught both youth and young adult classes. He served two years as the president of the area-wide youth rallies, organizing rallies in all of the participating churches. Because of his rapport with the local churches, he was solicited to fill the interims between pastors and to work with the leadership to bring in ministry to permanently fill that role. He has written and presented dramas, overseen praise and worship ministries, and helped direct youth ministries. He works side-by-side with his pastor in counseling as well as working with the leadership in all business decisions.

Dennis has filled the role of member, teacher, elder, associate pastor, interim pastor, and Board member. All of this experience has given him an unusual insight to the interactions of these offices within the church. The filling of interims has necessitated the understanding of the different church's offices, operations, and policies, as well as experienced him in working with the leadership and the Board of Directors of those churches. He has been placed in the position of interpreting the organization's documents as well as making changes, or even writing them.

One of the most enjoyable areas of Dennis' ministry has been the researching, developing, and teaching of different series from God's Word. Using the same analytical approach that has enabled him to finish the many projects he has supervised, he would compile the materials in such a way as to exhaust the topic, but present it in a fashion that all levels of audience could receive. One of those series, developed over many years and from a burden to see leadership undergirded, was the core for the material in this book.

Acknowledgments

My greatest appreciation to:

Pastors John Bosman, E.J. Dantin, Harold Eiland, Robert "Bob" Rutherford, Dub Williams. David Cook, President, International Bible College. Don Krider, Director, World Wide Ministries.

> For your review of this manuscript. For your input and your endorsement. For your continued support throughout this project. It was leaders like you that inspired this writing.

Deloris Williams.

> For your edit of the manuscript. I've learned to appreciate all the red ink.

Kerry Anderson, Attorney at Law.

> For all the question and answer sessions as I worked through Chapter 6.

Abundant Life Church Family.

> If every person who undertook a project had the backing and support I have with Pastor Bob, the leadership team, and this congregation, there would be no failures. Words fall short of expressing what my heart feels.

Friends and family.

> For all your heartfelt prayers and encouragement.

Introduction

Reason for this book.

Besides the salvation message, I do not think there are any other areas in God's Word that are more important than principles of leadership and an effective environment, or structure, for these to be displayed. Through the years of ministry I have seen the need for an understanding of what the scriptures say about leadership and leadership offices. I know there are principles, that if understood, will enable us to operate not only with the proper ethics, but with greater effectiveness in our ministry. Every time I would teach (or hear teaching) in these areas, I would feel that someone needed to put it in a book. I never dreamed that I would pick up the pen (or in my case the keyboard) to do so. Over the last year and a half, however, God helped me to see several needs in the church environment that brought me to the place where I knew that He was prompting me to do just that.

To understand ministries.

Every leader should understand where and how ministries in the church are supported in God's Word. I first became aware of how this need could exist as questions surfaced during my own studies; questions that I had never before thought to ask. They came as I prepared to minister a message dealing with leadership offices. A close friend, who had been my pastor a few years before, had invited me to minister an ordination service in his church. He was going to ordain several men into the positions of elder or deacon, and had asked me to preach on that subject. As I studied the responsibilities and qualifications for these two offices, I began to wonder about other offices in the church. I could find supporting scripture for deacons and elders, and how they were to be set into office. But, what about the pastor? I felt foolish to realize that I had never highlighted a scripture that said, "Set into office a leader and call him a pastor." (Not to mention trying to figure out where scripture supported associate

pastors, youth leaders, praise and worship leaders, sound operators, etc.) I began to feel a little better about myself, however,
when I discovered that other men of God had "never thought of
it just like that" either.

To understand church structure.

Secondly, there is the need to understand all of the structure
of the local church. My entire Christian life has been spent in
one type of church background. But even in that one background
I have dealt with churches that have different types of structure.
Typically that structure includes a pastor, elders and/or deacons,
and other ministries. But there are certain "legal" requirements
from the state and federal government that impacts the church's
structure as well. Some leaders, including pastors, understand
little about these requirements, and how they coordinate with the
day-to-day operations of the church, or with the scriptural
offices within the church. I have known people who accept that
they must have this structure, but don't really understand the
importance of, or how to operate in that same structure. Trying
to read the legal jargon and understand the requirements can be
somewhat intimidating, to say the least. So, God prompted me to
develop a better understanding of this area and to define the
pieces, and how they fit into everyday church life.

To understand principles of leadership.

Thirdly, I see an increasing need in God's Kingdom for men
who will "submit" to carrying out their roles of leadership with
integrity. One of the best ways to ensure that a leader operates
with integrity is to teach him proper leadership principles and
the importance of these to his ministry. I have known people in
ministry who wanted to do right, but just didn't have an understanding of what was expected or required of them in a
leadership role, and, it hurt their ministry. We study God's Word
to learn how to pray, learn how to preach, learn how to teach; I
could go on and on. So, why not study His Word not just to learn
how to lead, but to learn how to submit to authority of leader-

ship as well? I want to equip myself to be a leader, by understanding everything He has to say about the subject.

Burden for leadership.

And then, God began to increase within me a tremendous burden for leadership. Several times I had an opportunity to be in services where there were a number of pastors and leaders. As I would sit there looking out over the group, I would just begin to weep. I felt such a need for them to be ministered to, to be blessed, and to be encouraged. I ached to see them equipped with principles that would strengthen them. I wanted them to learn by ministry, not by trial and error as some of us have had to learn. I had the privilege of learning many important things under some Godly men. Things like how to prioritize my life, including my ministry. Things like not hurrying God's timing to accomplish what I had heard Him speak to me. Things like the importance of counsel. I began to ask God to help me be able to articulate to other leaders these things that I had learned over the years from the pastor's and associate pastor's seat. God not only did that, but He began to show me in Scripture how to support, and balance these principles. Here is where He has led me to pass along some of these important lessons.

God Given Confirmation.

It is <u>good</u> when God puts something in our heart that He is calling us to do. It is <u>great</u> when He brings confirmation. My confirmation came the first time I taught this study outline outside my home church. I was in the beginning stages of preparing the outline for this book, when a pastor asked me to teach the leadership material on four consecutive Wednesday nights. During the second night service, the Lord spoke something very clearly to me.

This church was in the second week of a three week fast, and God was doing marvelous things. The praise and worship led into a move of the Holy Spirit that was awesome. People began to humble themselves before God, and He was doing a tremendous work in their lives. I found myself asking God if a teaching like this needed to follow such a move of the Spirit. I supposed that the teaching would just be skipped that night. Certainly something more dynamic needed to take place than teaching! I would have been perfectly content if the pastor would have just preached!

It was about then that God spoke to my heart. He told me that He was removing things from peoples lives as they gave them up to Him. If these things were being taken out of their lives, then something needed to be put back in the void. That something was good Godly principles. This teaching was part of what He wanted to plant in the lives of those people! That was exciting enough, but then the pastor confirmed it! He stepped into the pulpit and let the people know that he felt God was still directing for me to teach!

God continued to confirm. I knew from the very beginning of the writing that I should solicit editing from several men. These were godly men, seasoned men that I had confidence would be fair and yet honest with me about what was written. At different stages of the writing I did just that, submitting the material to them to review for continuity, balance, and scriptural background. And then, I held my breath, waiting for their reply. You can only imagine my excitement as I received their confirmation that this material was not only needed, but timely as well!

And, word spread that I was writing this book. More and more the material came up in conversation, as people would inquire what I was writing about. Over and over they would express to me their interest in and need for having a comprehensive study of leadership material. I also began to realize that there was a lack of understanding of the terminology and requirements that the state and federal government imposed on the church body. This was perhaps the greatest confirmation of all, seeing that there was not only a need for, but an interest in the material the Lord was placing in my heart to compose.

15

Need for Structure.

Somewhere in the past (at least in the Pentecostal ranks where I grew up) the idea arose that structure hindered the move of God or lowered our level of spirituality. The church wanted so badly to be spiritual that many times it left behind teaching of <u>scripturally founded structure</u>. For so long we have taken this view:

Structure
vs.
Spiritual

when it should have been:

Structure
and
Spiritual

You don't have to be unstructured to be able to be spiritual. In fact, it very well may work the other way. When I look in the Bible, I see a God who is organized and desires order in His ranks. From the creation in Genesis through the activities of the Throne Room in Revelation I see a God who structures the events He controls. Events such as the instructions of the Tabernacle and its worship in Exodus stand as examples throughout His Word of His divine way of setting things in an order. He doesn't want us to be so structured that we cannot allow Him to lead and direct. <u>He does want us to be structured so that when He leads and directs we have the ability to carry out those plans efficiently.</u>

"Stir up your pure minds..."

The apostle Peter said that he wrote his epistles to "stir up" the "pure minds" of his readers (II Peter 3:1). That is my desire here. You may know many of the things I am going to cover, but I want to stir those things up in you again. If I were teaching from the pulpit, I would make challenges at this point. Intentionally I would say things that would command your attention, make you wonder how I was going to support and balance it. I would fire questions such as:

- What is scriptural structure?
- Does every church need this structure?
- How does a person know if he is a leader or not?
- What are the characteristics and responsibilities of leadership?
- What does the Bible say about leadership offices? Where?
- Why do we have a person over the church called a pastor? Where in scripture does it say to set a person in this position?
- Is it scriptural to have the other offices we see in a church? What about elders or deacons? What about associate pastors, youth leaders, choir directors, praise and worship leaders, or leaders of work details?
- Does the congregation have a role in this structure?
- What are "legal" requirements? How do we fit them into God's plan for the church?

And then I would tell you to be sure and listen to the rest of what I taught. So, now I must ask you to read the rest of what God has put in my heart to write. If you never minister in an area of leadership, this book still contains information that will help you understand your leaders, and your role under their leadership. If you are called to be a leader, the material covered here is critical information to equip you to successfully carry out that call.

My Aim!

There are two more things that I want to say before getting into the study. First, because many of the principles overlap several areas in the study, it is hard to fit them in one particular place. I have endeavored to place them where this study will have the best continuity with the least amount of repetition. In fact, I have restructured this study many times to find the best format.

This second point is one that **I wish I could raise my voice and command your attention while I say it**. I am not here to be corrective, nor comparative. I am not here to dictate any format or any changes. Nowhere am I trying to tell you to set in certain offices or to adopt a particular structure. (Don't copy me or anybody else for that matter.) The Lord has made it my responsibility to show you scriptural, proper leadership principles, and church structure that is effective in using these principles. He will have to direct you in how these can be supportive of the vision He has for you in your ministry. My aim is to provide a resource, a handbook, if you will, to aid in your study of these areas, offering definition and clarity. Your goal should be to prayerfully ask the Lord how these principles might help you to increase your effectiveness in the role He has called you to in His Kingdom.

May God richly bless you as you do!

Chapter 1

SCRIPTURAL STRUCTURE

Leadership Example

This study will draw from an Old Testament character -- Joshua. I want to take our main text from three verses that are brief and in the book of Joshua. I know that many may think it unusual to begin with Old Testament scriptures to teach on today's church structure. I also know that there are numerous examples in God's Word of good leaders. Joshua, however, stands out as one of the best. How many other leaders can say that they were so effective in their administration that every person under their care served the Lord until every leader they had trained had died (Josh. 24:31)? I think that before it is over, you will understand why I chose to use Joshua throughout this study.

But for those that need a little extra convincing that using old testament examples is applicable, remember what Paul wrote to the church at Corinth:

> *"1. Now all these things happened unto them (Israel) for ensamples (examples): and 2. they are written for our admonition, upon whom the ends of the world are come." -I Cor. 10:11*

Paul declared that Israel stands as an example. We have full-blown "felt-aids" in the Old Testament for us to use as operating examples in the New Testament! Secondly, Paul said that the Old Testament wasn't written in vain. Every principle in the New Testament is backed in the Old. We are here admonished to study the examples there along with the New Testament for clarity. Well, enough preaching from that soap-box. Let's look at our text:

And Joshua gathered all the tribes of Israel to Shechem, and called for the elders of Israel, and for their heads (some translations say "leaders"), and for their judges, and for their officers; and they presented themselves before God. -Joshua 24:1

And Joshua said unto all the people (Hebrew word implies "attendees"),... -Joshua 24:2 a

And Israel served the LORD all the days of Joshua, and all the days of the elders that overlived Joshua, and which had known all the works of the LORD, that he had done for Israel. - Joshua 24:31

Would you permit me to paraphrase these verses?

The leader (Joshua) called for all the leadership and they came (vs. 1). And this leader gave instructions to the congregation (Israel) through the leadership (vs. 2). This congregation served God until every member of the leadership team, raised up under this leader, was gone (vs. 31).

Proper Order.

Here we have our first hint of proper order. God chose to put into Joshua's heart a burden to see the people make a sure commitment to serve Him. Joshua needed to communicate that message to the people. But, remember, Joshua's congregation numbered several million! It would have been impossible for him to have effectively ministered that message to so many people. He needed help. So, Joshua used the tool that he had already proven many times before. He called his leadership teams together. A study of the text indicates that Joshua must have talked to those leaders in attendance, who in turn talked to the people under their individual care.

God chose to speak through a leader, to others involved in leadership, and then to the people. We must notice also, that the channel of communication must have gone both ways. We see several times that the people returned an answer to Joshua's questions. I must believe several million people did not talk to Joshua individually or together as a group. Surely, their reply came back to Joshua through the same leadership that Joshua had talked to in the beginning.

*God Speaks!

I have to take a parenthesis here and deal with an issue that has surfaced before when I taught this material. People have come to me after this lesson and said, "I thought God spoke to any New Testament believer." They were ready to discount what I was saying here because I was talking so strongly about God speaking through leadership. So that I am not misunderstood and lose a few readers, let me explain. If I were teaching this in a class I would, at this point, turn to the board and write:

God <u>does</u> speak to His people who will listen!

I know that God speaks to all believers who will hear Him. I am not saying that He will not speak to anyone else in the church because he has a leader, or leadership, over them. But, in this study I am talking about leadership structure as a unit. It is God's plan to give the primary directions, and responsibility for those plans being executed, to that person whom He has placed into a position of leadership and authority. Generally, this is the pastor. If the pastor is hearing from God, the directions that others hear from God will line up in support. When God speaks to others in the church, He will NEVER contradict what He has spoken to the pastor. I will deal with this subject in greater detail when I deal with leadership principles, but I know from experience that it must be touched on here at the beginning of this study as well.

Well, back to the study...

Elements of a proper organization.

We have seen in our study text that there are three elements that make up a proper structure or organization. At this point let's examine and relate them to our New Testament structure:

Study Text.	**New Testament Church.**
• A leader that God chooses to set in.	The pastor.
• Others in leadership who will be overseen by the leader	Elders, deacons, teachers, youth leaders, worship leaders, etc. overseen by the pastor.
• A people who will allow themselves to be led by God through these men.	The congregation.

In future chapters we will cover each of these three areas in detail and talk about how they should interact.

A "Common Sense" Look.

All three elements are necessary to complete a proper, healthy structure. Before getting theological, let's just take a moment for a good "common-sense" look.

- A pastor without leaders or people is not a pastor at all. Think about it. A person will have a hard time shepherding if he has no sheep.
- A pastor with people and without leaders is unhealthy. And for many reasons. This pastor has limited support and counsel without a leadership team. He has to shoulder all the responsibility alone. Because of this, it is difficult for the church to grow beyond his limitations. There is the danger of a pastor, without any leadership to work with, becoming totalitarian and unbalanced in his rule. Many times, a pastor will loose the "voice from the people" if he has no leadership to communicate their needs back to him. Good leadership should give the pastor a closer contact with the people.

I understand that infant churches may have an interim where this area of leadership is not established. I also know that pastors in small churches are sometimes limited in having people with leadership potential in their congregation. All care must be taken in these situations for the pastor to be open to leadership candidates as they are made available to him. During the interim, he must take guard against those dangers mentioned above.

- Leaders without a pastor are like a body with more than one head: it should not exist, and I find no support for this type of rule in the scriptures.
- People without leadership are only a crowd. Their direction is unsure, established only by the flow of those around them.

Structure.

If structured properly, the pieces of the organization should form an organization that is easily represented by the shape of a triangle. This structure will have a definite head, a firm base, and a mid-structure that connects the two. Even at this early stage it is easy to notice that it is the congregation that provides the basis and support for all of the leadership to operate upon. They are to carry the weight of providing a nurturing environment for the leadership team.

In its proper form, the structure's weight is easily supported. To see this principle more clearly, think of it as each person literally, physically carrying the weight of another. Since there are more people in the congregation layer than in the leadership

23

layer, each leader would have multiple people carrying him. The same principle would apply to the pastor as well. Clearly, the more people carrying another, the easier the load becomes for all. Inverted, one person would have to carry the weight of many. Certainly the leader and the leadership would stagger under such a load. Eventually the weight would exceed their ability to carry it.

This structure will have stability. Having more support at the bottom of the structure, it will have a strong base. It is solid in its design and cannot be easily toppled. Even if one or two were to fall, the overall stability of the structure will remain. Inverted, that is, built on the ministry or charisma of one person, the structure will only be stable as long as that one person is stable. If that person falls, the entire structure collapses with him.

It is uniform. The pastor, or the head of the structure, can more easily touch the mid-section, the leadership that supports him, than he can the entire congregation. Simply, he is dealing with a fewer number of people. This becomes increasingly more apparent as the church grows. The leadership body can communicate more effectively to the congregation because the ratio of leaders to the people is better.

Properly Placed.

It is not enough however, for this organization to be properly structured. As proper and scriptural as it may be, it can not succeed unless it aligns itself properly with God's full plan for structure. The following picture illustrates what I mean.

It is obvious by now that the structure we are talking about is the local church structure. This local body is also a part of the corporate body of Christ, the Church. The Lord desires to be the head of the Church, therefore the head of the local body as well. In fact, the scriptures teach that He cares for the Church as a husband should care for his wife.

And he is the head of the body, the church: who is the beginning, the firstborn from the dead; -Col. 1:18

Christ

Old Testament   *New Testament*

Leader
(Pastor)

Others in Leadership
(Elders, Deacons, Ministries)

**All the other people that
made up the nation of Israel**
(Congregation)

Jesus   *Apostles / Prophets*

*For the husband is the head of the wife, even as Christ
is the head of the Church: -Eph. 5:23*

Not only will he direct the church, He will protect it as well.
The pastor has authority over this body. He is the mouthpiece
(we will cover this more thoroughly in the chapter dealing with
the pastor). Yet, he will give account of how he has used this
authority when he stands before God (Heb. 13:17).

And then, the church must be set on the true foundation. The
Bible makes it clear that Jesus is the cornerstone of this founda-
tion. Just as a cornerstone is the beginning of and the strength to
the walls, Jesus is the beginning of and the strength to the
Gospels. No man laid this foundation, Christ laid it Himself.
Upon it the apostles and prophets were able to build.

*For other foundation can no man lay than that is laid,
which is Jesus Christ. -I Cor. 3:11*

*Now therefore ye are no more strangers and for-
eigners, but fellowcitizens with the saints, and of the
household of God; and are built upon the foundation*

of the apostles and prophets, Jesus Christ himself
being the chief corner stone. -Eph. 2:19,20

And upon it we are to build. Peter tells us that we are like "lively stones," built up a "spiritual house," and are to build upon this foundation that Jesus laid (I Peter 2).

Anyone who begins to build must first acquire the tools and materials necessary for the task. The same principle applies in the work God has called us to. We need to equip ourselves to be leaders. The following chapters minister principles of leadership. They will talk about offices of leadership and how they can interact with each other. They will define the necessary pieces of church structure. All of these things can become tools of our trade. Prayer and God's anointing will empower these tools.

I am reminded of Bezaleel in the 35th chapter of Exodus. Moses had just brought to the nation of Israel the commandments and instructions from God about how to build the Tabernacle. Bezaleel was to be one of the leaders of the workers. Verses 30 through 34 says that God knew him (called him by name), filled him with His Spirit, gave him wisdom, understanding, and knowledge about the work. Then God put in his heart the ability for him to teach the things that he knew to other men, who were equipped with wisdom and talents to accomplish different parts of the work. My desire is that you will pray, asking God to do the same for you as you study to become a leader.

Chapter 2

THE LEADERSHIP ROLE

The Team.

If we look at the diagram of church structure, that we drew in our last chapter, we realize that two-thirds of it involves leadership. For this reason we need to examine closely the leadership sections. In future chapters we will discuss the different offices of leadership, paying close attention to the qualifications for and the operations of each office. But, before we study each office independently, there are some principles that apply across the entire leadership spectrum. To be honest, this chapter was created by combining material from each of the other chapters. As I worked through them, I began to see that I could not isolate the principles to one area of leadership. I realize that some of the topics discussed here apply more directly to the pastor, however, the same principles also effect any member of the leadership **team**.

And team is a word that I do not use lightly. I have worked on many projects in my secular career, and I can distinctly point out those projects whose participants worked as a team. Those were the projects that ran smoothly, did not overburden any one participant, and accomplished the project's goals with the greatest ease. I might even add that these were the projects that were the most fun. These could be contrasted to those projects that, although the goals were eventually achieved, had to be endured because the participants could not pull together as a team. Someone has rightfully suggested that the word **TEAM** should say **T**ogether **E**verybody **A**ccomplishes **M**ore.

There is no place more important for the teamwork concept to be promoted than in the local church. We should be reminded, as was the church at Colosse, that we are **all** working to promote *one* body.

> *And let the peace of God rule in your hearts, to the which also ye are called in one body; and be ye thankful. -Col. 3:15*

Although the specific ministries differ, each should compliment the next to reach the common goal. It is evident in his writings that Paul understood this concept. He knew that he could not do everything alone, nor should he tear down another's accomplishments to promote his own. He teaches that we should all labor together, one carefully building upon the work of another.

> *For we are labourers together with God: ye are God's husbandry, ye are God's building. According to the grace of God which is given unto me, as a wise master-builder, I have laid the foundation, and another buildeth thereon. But let every man take heed how he buildeth thereupon. -I Cor. 3:9, 10*

> **About a year and a half ago I was honored to fill the position of interim pastor at a church and be involved in working with the leadership there to bring in a new pastor. The previous pastor had been there for about eight years and had been successful in establishing a foundation for future growth. One criteria the Lord put in our hearts was to know that the person who would come in as the new pastor would build on this foundation. We wanted a person who would continue to carry forth the vision and direction of the church, building on the previous pastor's accomplishments, instead of discarding them and starting over. The Lord allowed us to find such a man, and the church's growth today reflects his wisdom in building on another's foundation.*

It is comparative of a house being built. There is a need for an architect to provide a blueprint, a plan for the project. But, it is not enough for this same blueprint to be available to each worker; their efforts must be coordinated as well. The carpenter cannot raise a wall before those pouring the cement for the foundation are finished. Neither should he tear up the foundation to pour another just because he did not pour the first. The person that is going to hang the wallboard on the walls cannot do so before the carpenter frames them. The painter can not come before the wallboard is finished. Everything must be in order, building on the previous, and someone must orchestrate it all. For this reason a head contractor or carpenter is placed in charge of the workers.

God can cause ministries that He has placed together to flow together as well. He, as the Head Architect, has already furnished all the plans needed in His Word. It is the Blueprint. He then sets a person to be the "lead" contractor, the pastor. But He doesn't stop there. He can establish relationships between the workers. He can move on those involved to have the attitude and wisdom to work together to accomplish His work (see Exodus 31:1-11). When this happens, the team is not only coordinating their efforts, they are supporting, even complimenting, each other's ministry.

*In the last twelve years I have had the privilege of serving consecutively as associate pastor under two men whom I esteem very highly. These men are quite different from each other, yet God put our hearts together as only He can do. Many times I have stood in awe of how God coordinated our efforts, always leading both of us in the same direction. Whether He was directing us in a service by the move of His Spirit, or giving direction to each of us individually for messages we would preach in back-to-back services, it was evident that He had blended our ministries for His purpose. In addition, He helped us to support each other, encourage each other, make joint decisions, and remain in agreement. Nothing can replace the effectiveness of this kind of "team work".

The different areas, or offices, of leadership in the church should work together to form the type of team we are discussing. This team should support each other in the ministry of governments.

And God hath set some in the church, first apostles, secondarily prophets, thirdly teachers, after that miracles, then gifts of healings, helps, **governments**, diversities of tongues. -I Cor 12:28

The word used here for governments means "to guide," speaking of those who are in a position to act as guides in a local church. Its usage is one that denotes steering or pilotage, comparative of a captain steering a ship. This captain cannot sail the ship alone, but with an able crew, he is able to take the ship, with all aboard, to its destination. With a steady hand upon the "rudder," and God as the compass, the leadership team should be able to "pilot" the work of the local church, whether in fair weather or a storm, until they reach the final Harbor.

There is one thing that will surely destroy this team concept -- allowing ourselves to begin comparing ministries. Paul dealt with this problem in a later epistle to the church at Corinth.

> *For we dare not make ourselves of the number, or compare ourselves with some that commend themselves: but they measuring themselves by themselves, and comparing themselves among themselves, are not wise. -II Cor. 10:12*

Comparing ministries often breeds envies and jealousies, which left unchecked, will destroy a work. In any case a comparative attitude will soon damage working relationships. It is impossible to support or promote the ministry of a peer if we are using that peer as a benchmark to measure our own accomplishments. Instead of comparing and judging, leaders should strive to create and support an atmosphere of trust. A beautiful example of such trust in a working environment is found in Nehemiah 4:16, 17, and 21. Because of danger from their enemies, the Israelites found it necessary to post guards over the workers. Half of the men worked, while the other half protected them. Could you work on the construction knowing your safety was completely in the hands of a co-laborer? Could you stand guard, trusting someone else to accomplish the work that you had originally been assigned to do?

Called to Leadership.

Before discussing how leaders are "set in" or placed into office, I must cover a very important principle. There must be a

God-placed calling in a person's life to the area of leadership he is being placed. Man must not call them! <u>It is imperative that a person knows it is God who has called him to be in any position of leadership.</u> This begins with the pastor and extends to every area of ministry in the church. Some may have never given serious thought to callings being applicable to particular leadership areas, and others may so readily accept this principle that they might feel it is redundant to spend much time on the subject here. But, let me explain why I want to do so.

First, I have seen people who view leadership offices in much the same way they would view any secular office. They would award the office to a person based on their perception of that person's qualifications. While a person's qualifications are very important, they are not the total basis for placing that person into office. When a person meets the qualifications for a leadership office, and that person is solicited for that office, he should also know that it is God's desire for him to be active in that area of leadership before making the commitment. Otherwise, it becomes more of a job than a ministry.

Secondly, I have seen people who had a definite calling in their lives to a particular ministry, were effective in that area of ministry, but then were sidetracked into another area. There are different reasons why this happened. Some listened to what others encouraged them to do. Others pursued an area of ministry that they considered more appealing or more authoritative. Whatever the reason, they placed themselves in an area of ministry outside their true calling. Although God can bless them and use them, they may never be as effective as they could have been in the area God wanted them originally.

A calling is something that God places in the heart. It goes beyond logically thinking through a list of talents or abilities and deciding upon a particular role that has need for them. A calling creates an interest in what we are doing and a burning desire to be about doing it. If I love computers, for example, someone is not going to have to make me sit down at one. I will read about them, study them, develop skills on them, bring them up in conversation. My attention is drawn to anything that has to do with them. If I am called to a particular role of ministry, I will be much the same way towards it. I won't have to have someone continually motivating me to be busily involved.

Make your calling and election sure.

How would you like a promise that you will not fail in your ministry? God has given us one in His Word if we will make sure of two things -- our calling and our commitment (election to commit).

Wherefore the rather, brethren, give diligence to make your [calling and election sure]: for if ye do these things, ye shall never fall. -II Peter 1:10

I know that this scripture can be applied to God's calling us to salvation and our commitment to Him after repentance. But I also feel that it is applicable in ministry areas of our lives as well. First, we must be absolutely certain of His specific calling in our lives. If no other person ever recognizes that calling, we must still be sure of it. And once we are sure, we must then be completely surrendered to that calling. There can be no question about our commitment to fulfill our ministry.

When we come to that assurance, there will not be anything that can cause us to fail. This does not mean we will never make mistakes. But, it does mean that we can stand in the face of opposition, doing so in the confidence that we are there by His placing, and because we are, endure any test that comes our way. The heat of the battle, when opposition arises, is not the place to deal with doubts about being where God wants us to be. Settle this issue in your heart beforehand and know that if He placed you there, He won't leave you there alone. Instead of questions about going on, you can lean on His strength to get you through.

A perfect example of this is Paul's experience at Philippi (Acts 16). He had just been given a vision by God, a call to come to Macedonia. In the first Macedonian city that he preached in he was arrested, beaten, and thrown in jail. Instead of having to deal with thoughts of "I wonder if I was supposed to be here." or "What did I do wrong?," Paul was able to pray and sing praises from the depths of the dungeon.

I had not been in the ministry very long when a minister asked me a very peculiar question. He was a visiting minister at a fellowship in our church, and I had only met him that evening. We had not had much conversation, but as he came by me in the fellowship hall he paused long enough to ask me what area of ministry I was in. When I answered that I was the associate pastor, he asked, "Did God call you there or did you call yourself?" Becoming somewhat agitated, I replied that God had called me. That was the end of the conversation, and I had no idea why he asked such a thing. I admit that I really thought his question was out of place, and I was somewhat aggravated. But, the question would not go away. God used it to bring me to the place where I could say with absolute certainty that He had called me. I use that same question each time I consider a change in my ministry, "Is God calling or am I calling?" I do not move until I know He is. If you are thinking about entering into an area of leadership, I encourage you to come to the same certainty.

An episode in David's life shows us that sometimes those closest to us, even family, may not understand what God places in our hearts to do. In I Samuel 17:26 David inquires as to what would happen if a person was to defeat Israel's enemy, Goliath. We can almost see the indignation rise up in his heart! God's people would not be mocked this way! David begins to feel God's call to do something about the situation, only to be accused by his own brother. (Notice that Eliab had been rejected by God, I Sam. 16:7. Many times the one that has been refused by God is the one with the quickest criticism for what God is doing through the one chosen.) Eliab's accusations were completely off-base and erroneous. Yet, instead of getting into a bitter debate, spending precious time arguing the call, David simply stated, "Is there not a cause?". I want you to know. If God has truly placed a call in your life, there is a cause, and that is the only answer you need to give. You do not have to answer to family, friends, or foes. You do have to answer to God.

And in that answer, we may have to defend our position. If and when we do have to stand in defense, we can again follow Paul's example. In II Corinthians 10-13 he boldly and firmly vindicates his apostleship, never doubting that God gave him his authority. He knows God placed him where he is. He asks no man for validation. Yet Paul stops short of boasting or self-promotion. When we are confident in our call, we won't need to promote ourselves. God promotes those He calls.

The Lord placed a call in my life at an early age. This was a time when I was very immature in the Lord. I knew God wanted me to do something, but had little idea what that something was. That was okay, except for the fact that some well meaning "saints" thought they did know. My preaching style was somewhat evangelistic so over a period of time, they had me called as an evangelist, as a missionary, as this, and as that... Because I could not fulfill these callings, I began to feel there must be something wrong with my walk with God. This eventually led to discouragement, and for a while I even backed away from doing anything about my call to this ministry.

When I did return to the calling I was blessed to find Godly men who knew how to instruct me to wait for God's revealing of what His specific will was for my life. It was different than anyone had imagined. He called me to be an associate pastor. He led me through secular college, then gave me a secular job that would enable me to work with pastors in small churches without being a financial burden. I have filled the pulpit of other ministers in their absence; ministers who had no one else to minister and allow them to be gone. I was available to minister in the interim position when churches needed to be taken care of while God was placing a permanent pastor. These were important roles and no one else was there to fill them at the time.

I needed to be sure of that calling. For, in many eyes I had missed it by not going to a Bible college. Others voiced that surely God would "give me my own church" as soon as I was fully trained. Some still think that I just "haven't arrived" at the place where I can be used in a "full-time" ministry. These people stereotyped my ministry by their understanding (or misunderstanding) of other associate pastor positions. Many times I became discouraged, as others (often fellow ministers) treated me as "second-string." But, I knew that I had heard God, and I wasn't going to go out and do something He had not instructed me to do. Now, looking back, I see not only the effect this ministry had on these churches, I see its effect in my life. I don't think that I could have learned many of the principles that God wants in this book if I had not been in this type of ministry. I have been able to gain a view from the pulpit as pastor, from the leadership role as elder and associate pastor, and from the congregation as a member. I thank God I followed His lead.

Pursue your ministry only in the area or manner that God has ordained for you. Do not try to imitate another ministry. Do not worry about who is or is not fulfilling their call, worry about fulfilling the work God has called you to do. If we are to succeed in God's eyes, we must abide by the rules that He has handed us individually, as well as corporately.

And if a man also strive for masteries, yet is he not crowned, except he strive lawfully? -II Tim. 2:5

I therefore, the prisoner of the Lord, beseech you that ye walk worthy of the vocation wherewith ye are called, - Eph 4:1

A holy calling.

The calling placed in a person's life by God is not a frivolous thing. In fact, He makes it very clear that it is a holy, supernatural calling from God.

Who hath saved us, and called <us> with an holy calling... -II Tim. 1:9

It is not an attainment, it is the state that God places us. It is a privilege, an honor. Our calling should be devoted to God, placing upon us Divine demands. It is a calling that draws us toward the "high" standards God has placed on His work.

I press toward the mark for the prize of the high calling of God in Christ Jesus. -Phil 3:14

However, this calling does not place a person in a hierarchy that exalts him or exempts him from submitting to other leadership. Rather, this calling should place that person in an area of servanthood and accountability. We will discuss accountability and submission to leadership later in this chapter.

Called according to His purpose.

Let us remember that it is God who does the calling, and He sometimes does it differently than we would. He is no respecter of persons, and His criteria is somewhat different than ours might be. He doesn't call us according to our works. He doesn't call us because of what we have already done, or what we can do by ourselves in the future. He calls us according to what He knows we can accomplish through Him. He will never place a calling in our hearts that He is not ready and willing to equip us to accomplish.

Who hath saved us, and called <us> with an holy calling, not according to our works, but according to his own purpose and grace, which was given us in Christ Jesus before the world began, -II Tim 1:9

And we know that all things work together for good to them that love God, to them who are the called according to <his> purpose. -Rom. 8:28

There are illustrations in the Bible that show that God chooses differently. One is found in the anointing of David as king. Samuel was given instructions to fill his horn with oil and go to the house of Jesse the Beth-lehemite, with the purpose of anointing one of Jesse's sons king of Israel. As the oldest, Eliab, came before him, Samuel was sure that this was God's chosen, an act that would have followed tradition. God had this reply for Samuel,

Look not on his countenance, or on the height of his stature; because I have refused him: for the Lord seeth not as man seeth; for man looketh on the outward appearance, but the Lord looketh on the heart. -I Samuel 16:7

God had chosen David. It wasn't the traditional way of doing, but it was God's way.

Moses was chosen, even though he was eighty years old and had a problem with his speech. His self-attempt to be the deliverer had only created a murderer, yet God chose to use him to free Israel from bondage. Gideon was chosen as a warrior, even as he hid in the wine press from his enemies. Samson, a spoiled, whimsical brat, was one of the greatest judges in Old Testament history. Peter denied the Lord -- three times! -- yet, became one of the greatest apostles to the new Church. Paul, the destroyer of the church and persecutor of Christians, became one of the greatest figures in Bible history.

And what about the men that Jesus called! Just common men at best. No courser men could be found than the fishermen He added to His team. And He could not have called any more distasteful person than a tax collector! Yet, call them He did, along with others, to the great role of apostleship.

He could call you!

Wait on time and direction.

A person who is called into leadership must learn to wait on the proper time and direction for that ministry to be launched. Learning to wait is not an easy task. But, we must learn.

Having then gifts differing according to the grace that is given to us, whether prophecy, let us prophesy according to the proportion of faith; Or ministry, <u>let us wait on our ministering</u>: or he that teacheth, on teaching: Or he that exhorteth, on exhortation: he that giveth, let him do it with simplicity; he that ruleth, with diligence; he that showeth mercy, with cheerfulness. -Rom. 12:6-8

If God places a calling in a person's life, it will still be there when the timing is right for that person to step out into ministry. Launching the ministry any sooner may result in an underdeveloped ministry. A ministry prematurely birthed is similar to a baby prematurely birthed -- there may be a big head and a handicapped body.

Bottom line, knowing when to go means being able to be led by God. God introduced this concept to His people as a nation as He brought them out of Egypt. There His leading was in the form of a guiding cloud by day and a pillar of fire by night. The camp did not move until the cloud did, and then they went in the direction it lead. To move before the cloud led would have been stepping out ahead of God. Going in another direction than it led would have been moving away from His presence (Numbers 9:15-23). Staying when the cloud moved would result in being left behind. I have often wondered how many of the people argued with the cloud. How many times did they want to camp in an area they thought was better, travel in a different direction, or stay a little longer in a comfortable place? God knew the importance of His people learning to be led of Him.

Even great men like the Apostle Paul had to know how to be led by the Spirit. In the 16th chapter of Acts Paul receives direction from the Holy Spirit several times. First, Paul is not allowed to do something that he thought he should. The Spirit forbid him to minister in Asia and then stops his plans for turning into the area of Bithynia. Paul was not exactly sure what God wanted him to do at this point, but he was sure what God did not want. Many times knowing this is just as important as getting "go ahead" directions from God. Paul's listening to God's leading to NOT go into these areas, literally shaped the Christian world as we know it today! When it was God's time, He gave Paul the direction that he needed. God called him to Macedonia.

I remember a situation in my ministry when I really needed to hear what God wanted me to do. After praying for some time and not hearing an answer, I called a minister friend of mine for counsel. After listening to me for a few moments, he asked,

"What has God said for you to do?" I replied that I had not heard Him say anything specific. His next words were a gold mine, *"Well, maybe you can't hear God because He's not talking. At one time God gave you directions to do what you are currently doing. I suggest you keep doing **that** until He does say something to you, giving you some different direction."* Sure enough, in His own time God did give me leading. In the mean while, I enjoyed knowing that I was still where He wanted me.

I suppose the point that I am trying to drive home is this. We don't always know where we are going, but we do know who to follow! As long as we are hearing what God says, and are obedient, we cannot go wrong.

Looking unto Jesus the author and finisher of our faith;... -Heb 12:2

Many times, the timing of God leading us out into the field of ministry may be contingent on our being prepared to go out. In other words, our being used may be dependent on our being taught. God knows if we are mature enough to be sent out. This maturity is not just in the knowledge of His Word, but also includes our learning all the leadership principles that He knows we need. In this sense, we can have an affect on the length of time we have to wait. If we commit to allowing Him to mature us quickly, we may shorten the training period. If our commitment is lacking, this process may take longer. Paul describes the concept of this principle as an heir that, although he owns all, is no more than a servant because he is still childlike. He can not tend to the business at hand because of the lack of maturity.

Now I say, That the heir, as long as he is a child, differeth nothing from a servant, though he be lord of all; But is under tutors and governors until the time appointed of the father. -Gal. 4:1-2

There is another reason for God to have us on hold that may not be quite so obvious. We may be prepared to minister what we have received, but those to be ministered to may not be ready to receive it. God may be making preparation in other areas so that the ministry that He has given us can be the most effectively received. Seed falling on unprepared ground will give little harvest.

So while waiting on God's green-light, use the time to continue preparing.

It has also been my experience that God will give confirmation to a person He is speaking to. But, we need to be careful in this area not to get the "cart before the horse." Let me be careful not to be misunderstood. There is nothing wrong with getting God-given confirmation from someone else. When God gives confirmation that we are doing what He desires, it is a great comfort. However, sometimes we find ourselves wanting someone else to "give us a word" of direction or timing before we have really allowed God to speak to us. We can desire this because it takes the responsibility from us and places it on the person giving the advice. We need to allow God to *lead* us by His Spirit, and then *confirm* it by other means. Confirmation usually follows God having already spoken to a person's heart. Again, it is His plan that His children know how to be led by Him.

> *For as many as are led by the Spirit of God, they are the sons of God. -Rom 8:14*

*At one point in my ministry I needed to make a decision and I knew that God had been talking to me about what I should do. It was an important step in my life, but I was fairly sure that I had His direction. However, I started praying for God to put it into someone's heart to tell me that I was right. After service one evening, I got in my car, somewhat disappointed that nothing dynamic had happened to confirm my decision. When I started the car, the radio was on, tuned to my favorite Christian station. Someone was preaching on how to be led of God and posed this question, "Do you want to be people lead, or do you want to be Spirit lead?" It hit me right in the heart! I quickly made sure God knew I wanted to be Spirit lead, and took the first step to do what I had heard Him direct. Guess what! Almost immediately

after having made the commitment God gave me confirmation in such a way that I could not doubt! Although He doesn't always wait until we move to send confirmation, this time He knew I needed to learn a lesson.

Now let me make clear this point. Confirmation means that we know to go ahead with what God has put in our hearts to do. It does not mean that we will know all the details about what we lies ahead of us. Our instructions might be similar to Samuel's in I Samuel 16:1,3. God said to 1. Fill his horn with oil, 2. Go, 3. I will show you what to do. We need our horn (authority) filled with the oil (power of Holy Spirit) while we are preparing to go out. We then go out on the authority of God's call. We will receive our instructions as the need for God to reveal them to us arises. I think that sometimes He knows that if we knew the details of everything that was ahead of us, we might not go.

There is a principle that my pastor, Bob Rutherford, has stressed to me over the years. There will be a distinguishable feeling of peace in a person's heart when they are where they need to be, or when they have reached the decision God wanted. I have learned to recognize that peace, and I will not go ahead with a decision until I feel this peace in it.

Let me make one more point about this waiting period. While we wait, we may need to be careful how much we talk about what God is dealing with us about. I am not talking about excluding going to a pastor for counsel. We need to allow our pastor to be a part of our entire decision making process. I am talking about prematurely announcing what is going on in our hearts. We may announce something we have not heard clearly, and then have to retract what we said. This could give the appearance that we are not stable in our decision. Too long of a span between the announcement and action might cause people to doubt we were actually called. Or, we may just need to let God do it without a lot of fan-fare. Joseph learned this lesson the hard way. God was in his dreams and the events God showed him came to pass, including the fact that family would eventually have to give honor to him. But neither his brothers nor his father understood these things when Joseph announced them (Genesis 37), and his announcements caused him a lot of trouble.

Setting Leaders into Office.

I must discuss the setting of leaders into office in two parts. I want to talk about the office of pastor and then talk about the other leadership roles under the pastor's care.

Pastor must be God placed.

Joshua serves as a prime example of how God wants to place a leader over the people.

And Moses spake unto the LORD, saying, <u>Let the LORD, the God of the spirits of all flesh, set a man over the congregation,</u> Which may go out before them, and which may go in before them, and which may lead them out, and which may bring them in; that the congregation of the LORD be not as sheep which have no shepherd. And the LORD said unto Moses, Take thee Joshua the son of Nun, a man in whom <is> the spirit, and lay thine hand upon him; And set him before Eleazar the priest, and before all the congregation; and give him a charge in their sight. And thou shalt put <some> of thine honour upon him, that all the congregation of the children of Israel may be obedient. And he shall stand before Eleazar the priest, who shall ask <counsel> for him after the judgment of Urim before the LORD: at his word shall they go out, and at his word they shall come in, <both> he, and all the children of Israel with him, even all the congregation. And Moses did as the LORD commanded him: and he took Joshua, and set him before Eleazar the priest, and before all the congrega-tion: And he laid his hands upon him, and gave him a charge, as the LORD commanded by the hand of Moses. -Numbers 27:15-23

We see some interesting points in this passage of scripture. First, Moses asked the Lord to set the person over the nation that He wanted. Secondly, Moses listened to God's direction in choosing this person. Thirdly, he brought Joshua before the leadership and the congregation, laid his hands on Joshua, and gave him a charge from God.

I do not believe in voting a pastor into office based on popular nomination and vote. I do not believe in conducting the business of placing a pastor into office as one would to replace a CEO in secular business, rather I believe it is a two-fold process. First, God must speak to the pastor to come to that local body, and place within him a burden for those people that will be under his care. Secondly, the leadership of the local body must have received direction from God that this is THE person for the job, and must be able to recommend this person to the congregation with total confidence that God has ordained his being there.

*I had been filling the associate pastor position in a church for several years when God began to deal with me about moving to another church in my home town and closer to where we lived. The Lord confirmed the move in several ways, but one was in a way that has remained a lesson to me. He moved my burden. I was aware that God had given me a burden, a pastor's heart if you will, for the people where I was pastoring. But I began to realize that the burden for those people had changed. I still loved them, and cared for them (I do to this day), but the "shepherding" burden was not there. Instead, in the next few weeks, as I discussed this with my pastor and prayerfully waited on God's timing, I found myself thinking more and more about the people in the church where I was going. I felt a burden for them growing, and yet I did not know them well enough for this to have grown out of relationship.

*I realize now that God had released me from the burden of pastoring one congregation and had placed in my heart the burden for another. It wasn't something that I had developed consciously, but rather a work that God had done in my heart. Another pastor related a similar incident to me. He said that as

God was directing him to pastor another church, he began to realize that it felt as if he was visiting the church he was currently attending, and he needed to hurry and get "back home" to the church he was going to. He said that he realized that God had literally changed his focus or "burden" for the people even before he could physically make the move.

*God alone has the ability to supernaturally place such a love and care for a people that you have had limited exposure to. This love and care, this burden, is what makes you a pastor at heart. It is the drive that causes you to shepherd them.

*Oh, by the way, I didn't have to call the pastor at the church I was going to and tell him God sent me there to be in the ministry. When I talked to him and told him we were being led to begin attending church there, he confirmed our direction by telling us that the Lord had already spoken to him that we were coming. He offered a co-pastor's position, and we have been there ever since.

Both of these are critical. There will be trying times sooner or later in any pastorate. It is during these times that a pastor must know absolutely that it is God's will for him to be there. It is equally important during these times that the leadership and the congregation be able to not question their decision in placing him.

We can use some of the same tools or vehicles that the secular world uses in the process of selecting a pastor. There is nothing wrong with resumes, tapes, or interviews. These should be used as a means of becoming acquainted with candidates. BUT, while becoming acquainted with the candidates, there is no substitute for prayer, fasting, and waiting on God's direction. I know from experience that God can, and will, bring the leadership body to a place of agreement in confirmation of the man God wants for their pastor. I also know the leadership can be instrumental in the congregation's approval of this decision.

(I know that some churches are under the auspices of an organization that will aid them in the process of placing a pastor. Whatever the level of decision, however, these principles of knowing God's direction are applicable. When we discuss elders later in this book, we will talk about their responsibility to the local body in this process. If and how other leaders, the Board of Directors, or outside presbytery, play a role in this decision process should be defined as well. The Constitution and Bylaws of the church is the proper place for such definition. In fact, the entire process of bringing in a pastor, and who is responsible for each piece of the process, should be clearly defined there. See chapter 6)

The leadership body should follow the guidelines from our scripture text above. 1. They should go to God in prayer, asking Him to set a man over the congregation. 2. Then they must listen for His answer. This listening time is the time that they must become acquainted with candidates. 3. When the leadership body is in agreement that they have God's direction, they should present this person to the congregation. 4. When accepted, this person should be "set into office" before the congregation by the laying on of hands. He should accept a Godly charge to faithfully fulfill the role that God has placed him in.

A Theocracy.

We must keep in mind that the Church was never designed to be a democracy, nor was it designed to be a dictatorial form. God's plan was that the Church be a *theocracy*. This is defined as a form of government in which God or a deity is recognized as the supreme ruler. God is THE supreme ruler, and the Holy Spirit is His communication channel. It is vital that God place a man over the people that He alone knows will be a person who will stand in that specific place of leadership and allow God to direct him. The rules of leadership are static. They are God's Word. The strategies in carrying out these rules may change from location to location to be effective and must be God implemented through a man placed as pastor. Man simply does not have the ability to place a person to do this; God does.

Let me explain by giving an illustration that God showed me. When I teach this in a group, I ask a person to stand. I then ask that person to dictate to me every future detail of the church

-- every ministry, every decision, every problem, every solution, etc. for the next 10 years. Of course, he is not able to do so. Point proven. God does know all these things. In addition, He knows the ability of the man he elects. He will place a person there who can carry out His direction in all these circumstances.

Placing other Leaders.

It is interesting in the Bible to see how other ministries are to be placed. God has clearly defined the qualifications for the offices of leadership in His Word. These qualifications are the tools that a pastor should use to set people into the offices, and use to uphold the integrity of offices once they have been filled. We see in the book of Acts that it was the leadership's responsibility to make the appointments to fill the offices. I believe it is the pastor's responsibility to appoint leadership in the local body, as God gives direction. He would be wise to use the counsel of his other leaders in the placing of these ministries. This whole process must be done with much prayer, fasting, and waiting on God. (We see the old testament principle of laying hands upon the person and commending them to the Lord in their ministry carried into the new testament.)

Wherefore, brethren, look ye out among you seven men of honest report, full of the Holy Ghost and wisdom, whom we may appoint over this business. But we will give ourselves continually to prayer, and to the ministry of the word. And the saying pleased the whole multitude: and they chose Stephen, a man full of faith and of the Holy Ghost, and Philip, and Prochorus, and Nicanor, and Timon, and Parmenas, and Nicolas a proselyte of Antioch: Whom they set before the apostles: and when they had prayed, they laid <their> hands on them. -Acts 6:3-6

For this cause left I thee in Crete, that thou shouldest set in order the things that are wanting, and ordain elders in every city, as I had appointed thee: -Titus 1:5

And when they had ordained them elders in every church, and had prayed with fasting, they commended them to the Lord, on whom they believed. -Acts 14:23

It is critical that leadership be set in and harmonized while everything is going well. While all is "smooth sailing" attention should be given to praying, fasting, hearing from God, and establishing the leadership team. All decisions about roles, responsibilities, and structure should be decided on and <u>documented</u> while all are in harmony. (This document should be the church's Constitution and By-Laws, or operating procedure. It is critical that this documentation be done. I will discuss this importance in chapter 6, dealing with church government.) It is during this time that the leadership team(s) should learn to work together. Solidness here will give stability when a crisis hits.

Let me include another detail about appointing leadership. I think you already know that I feel the most important thing is hearing from God. If He clearly speaks to you to do something then do it! But, let me add that it is generally a good idea not to be too hasty in setting someone new to you into leadership. Time is not *the* qualifier for setting in leadership altogether, *but*, it will allow God to confirm what He has put in your heart about that person. Usually, a period of time is necessary for some of the qualifications for leadership to be made evident in a person's life. Also, it will take some time for that person to prove his commitment to the Lord and to the local church. I know that there are circumstances, such as knowing a person prior to his coming to the church that may allow deviation from these guidelines. But generally these guidelines are worth having, and if for no other reason than to adhere to them consistently, you may want to wait an appropriate length of time before giving a person an office.

It is a good practice to have pre-defined criteria for a person to meet <u>before</u> he can fill a leadership role in the local church. This will allow you guidelines to operate by, providing consistency in decisions and operations. Much thought and prayer should be given to setting this criteria. Once it is in place, do not compromise it. If one exception to these rules is allowed, it creates the potential for all of the guidelines to be voided. (The "you did it for him why can't you do it for me" problem.) **If the Holy Spirit leads you to set in guidelines, He will not lead you to violate them.** Consistency in application of this criteria will play a key role in success of administration.

Do not place a person in office to try to get them to start meeting this criteria. They need to be established and meeting this criteria, as well as the qualifications for the particular office of ministry, **before** being given the position. (A good example: "...look ye out among you seven men of honest report, full of the Holy Ghost and wisdom, whom ye many appoint over this business." Acts 6:3) If a person cannot be set in because he does not meet the criteria, use the guidelines of the criteria to work with that person to bring him to the place where he is qualified. Let me give an example. My son who is eleven years of age loves to drive our lawn tractor. He even thinks that he has reached the place where he could mow with no supervision from his father. I know, however, that his ability is limited at this point to driving the tractor with close supervision and without the mower deck engaged. Although he fusses, I know it would be dangerous to give in and allow him to have his way. But, I also know that soon, with continued training and experience, he will be able to assume the responsibility of mowing the yard. It's my responsibility as his father to train, encourage, and recognize when that time comes.

An incumbent who is faltering needs to be handled with much care. Every step should be taken to encourage and correct. If this cannot be accomplished, wisdom, along with the office qualifications should be used in determining whether that person can continue to fill that leadership role, or when he should be dismissed. Again, having clear, established pre-set guidelines will enable you to deal with these matters without valid criticism.

In our local church we have adopted this criteria that a person must meet before they can be considered for a leadership position.

- *A Christian who displays the love of God and obedience to the Gospel of Christ.*

- *A person who knows that God has specifically placed them at this church, understands and embraces the Tenets of Faith of the church, and has expressed to the leadership that they want to become a member.*
- *A person who faithfully supports the church in attendance.*
- *A person who faithfully supports the church in tithing.*
- *A person who faithfully supports the church in prayer.*
- *A person who faithfully supports the leadership in carrying out the vision and direction of the church.*
- *A person who knows God has called him to that specific area of ministry, and meets the qualifications for that ministry. (There are pre-set criteria for the specific area of ministry.)*

Launching Ministries.

The phrase "launching ministries" implies the sending <u>out</u> of ministries, I am going to teach on some important principles about the launching phase of ministry from an example that shows ministries leaving, or going out from, the local church. But we know that there are ministries that are "launched," or started, in the local church and remain as ministries inside the local church. No matter how much "going out" we do (or do not do) the principles we will discuss here are just as applicable. The example I am referring to is from the 13th and 14th chapters of Acts, the report of Paul and Barnabas in their first missionary journey. It not only shows some important principles, but the proper order to apply these principles.

Verse one covers the first point. Paul and Barnabas **were called of God to minister** the Gospel. We certainly know the story of Paul's conversion and calling from the 9th chapter. Barnabas emerges in the Book of Acts as a disciple in whom the Church placed much trust. Here, in this first verse, we see both are listed with the prophets and teachers. I think that I have said enough in this chapter about being called to ministry, so let's move on to point two.

They ministered to the Lord, verse two tells us. We talk so often about the Lord ministering to us, but how do we minister to Him? The particular Greek word used here was also used in Paul's day to signify "supplying service to a public office at one's own cost." It speaks of our giving everything we have in service, in our case, to Him. I tend to think it encompasses everything about our relationship with God as well as a commitment to the ministry He has called us to. I believe Paul and Barnabas prayed, and sought God. I believe they sang praises and worshipped Him. I believe they had fellowship with other believers. I believe they taught and preached His Word. I believe this is how they ministered to the Lord! Staying busy ministering to the Lord will make any wait seem much shorter.

And **they fasted.** I don't think we would be to far afield to suggest that not only did they abstain from food, they used the opportunity to pray and seek God for direction. The mere fact that the next thing that happens is the Holy Spirit giving direction seems to suggest that they were seeking it. It has been my observation that when a person is desirous enough to fast, they usually have a need to hear from God, and are serious enough to seek Him for that need. Notice that they fasted and prayed while ministering to the Lord and while waiting on His direction. Notice also that they fasted and prayed as they commissioned and sent out Paul and Barnabas. It seems that Someone wants us to see the importance fasting and praying plays in ministries being started.

And then **the Lord**, through His Holy Spirit, **spoke**, giving direction. I don't know how long they waited there before He spoke. I don't know how He spoke. What is important is that Paul and Barnabas did not go out on their own without His direction. As we said earlier in this chapter, it is important to wait on His time and direction. I also get the idea that the Holy Spirit did not give them all the details at once. In verse four we see that they were "sent forth by the Holy Ghost." I get the impression that God may have continued to give them directions even as they were taking steps to do what God had spoke to them in verse two.

They were sent on their way by the people. Verse three says that the people were involved in the fasting and prayer as well as Paul and Barnabas. It also says that they laid their hands on them as they sent them away. There is much involved in this Biblical principle, but let me simply say here that I believe it shows the people's desire to be a part of what Paul and Barnabas were doing. A principle behind the "laying on of hands" was the identification on the part of the one who did it with the person upon whom the hands were laid. In other words, Paul and Barnabas went out with the "backing" of the saints at Antioch. Wherever they were, they had the knowledge that others were supporting them, praying for them, and eager to hear what they had accomplished. I cannot stress enough the importance of every person in ministry having this type of support. We will discuss this subject of having "backing and covering" again in this chapter.

We must go to the 14th chapter to find the next two points. In verses 26 and 27 we see that Paul and Barnabas return to Antioch after their missionary journey and give a full account of all that God had accomplished for them on their journey. **There has to be accountability**. I know we will be held accountable to God. Jesus made very clear His position on accountability when He taught the story of the servants and the talents in the 25th chapter of Matthew. I also believe that we need to be able to give account to those who support us. If men of such caliber as Paul and Barnabas felt the importance to give a report, I think that we would be wise to consider doing the same. I know this; I would be hesitant to continue my support for a ministry I never heard from.

In the last verse of chapter 14 we find that Paul and Barnabas stayed a long time in Antioch. In the next chapter we find that once again they were busy about God's work while there. This they did until Paul felt the leading to launch out on his second journey. Looks a lot like this story is starting again at point two. **The cycle starts over**. There will be many such cycles in the life of a ministry. And a healthy ministry will be one that doesn't try to skip some of the steps.

Hindrances to Ministry

From time to time in my ministry as a pastor, the Lord has burdened me with a message that, if given the choice, I would not have ministered. I do not like having to deal in areas of correction or with topics that deal with reparation. But, they have to be preached. I do not like dealing with the negative. But, sometimes, knowing the results of wrong behavior can give us the wisdom to avoid it. With this state of heart I must warn of some conditions that will hinder a ministry.

I am not even sure where I first heard this list of hindrances taught. As I began to write this book, all I had was the list as they are found in Leviticus chapter 21 verses 17 through 20. I filled in the rest with material taken from the tapes where I recently ministered these principles to our local congregation. Here the hindrances are listed as physical disqualifications to the priesthood, so we might ask, "Did God give these disqualifications because He was being unfair to the handicapped?" I think not. Nor do we find any evidence in the New Testament that physical handicaps limit His calling people to the ministry. He did know that these conditions would hinder the priest of the Old Testament from fulfilling his duties, as physically stringent as they could be. And He also knew that these would serve as examples of spiritual hindrances found in a Christian walk today.

I will list the disqualifications found in Leviticus one by one and offer a brief thought of the application to ministries today. Remember, the key word is hindrances. These things may not drag us down into sin, they may not keep us from ministering, yet they will limit us from being able to minister at our fullest capacity. As you read these, don't focus on "Wow, here are 11 things that are going to get me." rather on "I'm going to be aware of these things and guard against them ever being allowed to hinder me."

1. A blind man: A person who cannot see. This speaks of that person who has no spiritual sight, or vision, at all. We must have a vision of what God is wanting us to accomplish.

Where there is no vision, the people perish:..... -Prov 29:18

The world has latched onto this concept. Most businesses today recognize the necessity of having a vision, or as they would call it, a mission statement. All of the company's activities must focus on supporting their overall mission. This is not a new concept to God. In the Church, there are three areas in which we must understand what the vision is.

The first is in the local church. We need to understand what it is that God wants to accomplish through our local church, and then be willing to support seeing that vision carried out. This is probably one of the most important principles in being a part of a local church. When God leads us to one, we must know that we are willing to support what He is doing in it. In fact, supporting the vision is one of the criteria that a church should list for its membership requirements. A person can be faithful in attendance and faithful in tithing, but if they are unable to support the vision and direction of the church they will continually be at odds with the leadership and can reek havoc in a local body.

The second vision that we must have is the one God wants for the Corporate Church Body. What is the goal? Just to reach heaven? To build a bunch of big churches around the world? No! The purpose of the Church is to make ready the Bride of Christ. And this vision is all encompassing. It includes seeing the Gospel spread, it includes people being saved and birthed into the Kingdom, it includes ministry that will sanctify those people and ready them for the Lord. We need, as part of this vision, to understand how our local church body integrates into the activities of the corporate Body.

And then, we must have a vision for our personal walk. No matter how large or how insignificant we might think our ministry is, we need to understand what it is that God wants us to do. We then must ask these questions, "How does our ministry support the vision of the local body? How does this ministry promote the vision for the Church?"

We must also be able to make that vision available to others.

And the LORD answered me, and said, Write the vision, and make it plain upon tables, that he may run that readeth it. -Hab. 2:2

People ought to know what we are about! I need to tell them about Dennis Moses. About his love for God. About his lifestyle, his convictions, his relationship with God. I need to let them understand what my local church is all about. How it functions. Why it's there. And then, I need to let them know about God's plan for His Church.

2. A lame man: A person who can not easily get around. He can go (about the work of the ministry), but it is an inconvenience. There are those who are extremely gifted with talents, yet they do not want to commit to using their talents because of the demands it will make on them. Doing what God has equipped them to do just might inconvenience their lifestyle. Consequently, because it does, they may not even go.

When we set limits on how much we will or will not do for the Lord because of the inconvenience it may cause us, we are "lame" in our work for the Lord. (And if I might play on words, whatever reasons we voice to justify not using our abilities are going to be "lame" excuses before God.) You want to know what Jesus thinks about a person who would squander a God-given talent? He referred to the man as "wicked and slothful" (Matt. 25:14-29). That is mighty strong language, but admittedly this man knew what his Master would demand of his talent and instead of using it, laid it aside.

God expects a return. Just tally up what He has invested in you. He invested His Son's death in you, His Holy Spirit in you, a relationship in you, a calling in you, and talents in you. He then invests His anointing upon you. What He demands is a return of 100%. Anything short of that is "lame."

3. A flat nose: A person who has no scent discernment (smell). Many Christians today lack spiritual discernment, that is, an acuteness of judgment and understanding of the things of God.

We find that God gives the Christian an ability to understand or discern the Word of God.

But the natural man receiveth not the things of the Spirit of God: for they are foolishness unto him: neither can he know them, because they are spiritually discerned. -I Cor 2:14

Discernment grows as we study God's Word and learn more about His ways through a relationship with Him. One of the best ways for me to discern whether something is good or bad is to be able to know whether or not it lines up with His Word. I should also be able to tell if something is amiss, if it is contrary to the nature of Christ within me. As we mature our ability to discern is honed. The more we grow, the more we learn. The more we use these senses, the more acute they become. Let me give an example. How many of us can tell the difference, discern if you will, between a pone of cornbread in the oven and a cake baking? We weren't born with this ability; we learned it by having experienced those smells before. Experience in the things of God strengthens our spiritual discernment in much the same way.

*But strong meat belongeth to them that are of full age, even those who by **reason of use** have their senses exercised to discern both good and evil. –Heb. 5:14*

There is one other area of discernment that goes beyond what we have discussed so far. We can receive the gift of discerning spirits. This gift goes beyond our ability to learn to discern by natural senses. It is the Spirit-empowered ability to know the nature of spirits. It is the ability to recognize what is of God and what is not, not by anything we might be able to "put our finger on," but because the Holy Spirit has shown us.

To another the working of miracles; to another prophecy; to another discerning of spirits... -I Cor 12:10

There is one sure way to dull your discernment. Mixing with the world and becoming callused to the sensitivity to God's Spirit within us will surely lessen our ability to discern.

4. Superfluous: A person having an excess (in the physical an excess of members, i.e. six fingers or six toes, etc.) This speaks of a person who is superficial, or a novice and is looking only for gain for himself. Sadly, the church world has had its share of those who would profit at the expense of the ministry.

Not a novice, lest being lifted up with pride he fall into the condemnation of the devil. -I Tim 3:6

Now, God doesn't mind us being blessed. He wants us to prosper. He doesn't mind us owning anything, so long as it doesn't own us. However, His purpose for equipping us in the ministry is not for us to see how much we can gain by it. Jesus himself spoke of a man who laid treasures up for himself and at the same time was negligent toward God.

But God said unto him, Thou fool, this night thy soul shall be required of thee: then whose shall those things be, which thou hast provided? So is he that layeth up treasure for himself, and is not rich toward God. -Luke 12:20-21

When talking about a man denying himself, taking up his cross and following him, Jesus finished with this statement:

For what is a man profited, if he shall gain the whole world, and lose his own soul? or what shall a man give in exchange for his soul? -Mat 16:26

But, this attitude is not limited to a person building up assets. It includes the attitude of "look what I've done." The title means more than the work to this person. Jesus paints another vivid picture of this for us in the parable of the Pharisee and the publican in Luke 18. Although the Pharisee rehearsed all the things he took pride in having done, his reward could not stand in the presence of a publican who humbly presented himself to God.

5. Broken footed: A person who has an impaired spiritual walk. This is different than the person in point two who doesn't want to commit to going. This is the person who is active, who goes about the work he is called to, but who allows things in his life that just hinder his ability to walk -- things that are always tripping him up. He continues to hang on to little things, hidden things, that appease the flesh.

Paul called these the sins that easily set us back (Heb. 12:1). They continue to trip us up. No one may ever see them. No one may ever know these things exist in our lives. But God knows they are there, and He may also know that until they are removed, He cannot allow us to move forward into more responsibility.

6. Broken handed: A person who can not do (the tasks of the ministry that he is called to do). Now, how can that be? We are most familiar with the scripture that says we can do all things through Christ who strengthens us (Phil. 4:13). So how can a person "not do?" It has to be either that he will not do or he is doing in his own abilities, leaving God out of the picture, and is limited.

In the first chapter of II Peter the writer gives us a list of virtues that we are to diligently add to our Christian character. In verse 8 he tells us that if these things are in us we will never be barren or unfruitful in the knowledge of our Lord, and in verse 10, if we add making our calling and commitment sure along with these things, we will never fail. But in the 9th verse, he says that if these things are lacking, we "cannot" see, implying that we will have no vision to carry out the work. There is some-thing interesting about this word "cannot." The word implies an intentional shutting of the eyes. The person could see if he wanted to, but has made the decision not to be attentive, inten-tionally shutting his eyes to avoid seeing things that need to be done. It is a self imposed "cannot" do.

God has made every provision necessary for our Christian walk. He has given instructions in His Word, and then empowered us with His Spirit. If we cannot put our hands to the task and see things accomplished for Him, it is not because of His limitations.

As I was praying for a person after a service, the Lord put something in my heart to share with her. Her request for prayer was to have the ability to accomplish what she knew the Lord had called her to do. She felt like she did not have the necessary talents to see it done. The Lord showed me that the desire had been placed in her heart by Him. He then wanted her to know that if he placed that desire in her, He would supply the means to see that work accomplished. Let me give another example. Wouldn't it be foolish if I told my son to go and mow the yard, and then refuse to let him use the mower? "I'm going to punish you if it's not mowed by dark, but I'm not going to let you have the tools to do it." No, God doesn't operate that way either. He equips those whom He calls.

7.Crookbacked: A person who is burdened down by things. I am not talking about God-given burdens for people under our care or for our ministry, nor am I talking about sin in our lives. I am talking about allowing ourselves to be caught up in the affairs of this world to the point where we are overwhelmed, and it affects our Christian walk. Jesus warned that there are those in the religious arena who would impose their legalism, causing our walk to be once again burdened (Matt. 23:4). But, we can take on so many responsibilities in our fast paced life that we become overburdened as well. So often we have so many things going on at the same time we find ourselves in the "putting out fires" syndrome. That is, we can't finish anything because we are too strung out just trying to keep everything going. Mark gives us this warning:

And the cares of this world, and the deceitfulness of riches, and the lusts of other things entering in, choke the word, and it becometh unfruitful. -Mark 4:19

and Paul writes to Timothy warning him to be careful for:

No man that warreth entangleth himself with the affairs of this life; that he may please him who hath chosen him to be a soldier. -II Tim 2:4

We are then further admonished to "lay aside every weight" (Heb. 12:1) and then to help one another by helping "bear one another's burdens" (Gal. 6:2). Jesus promised us an easy yoke and a light burden if we would but go to Him (Matt. 11:28, 30).

Sometimes we just have to stop. and decide which of the many things going on in our lives the Lord wants us to focus on. This is where we see the importance of understanding the *Relationships and Priorities* section of this chapter.

8. Dwarf: A person who is growth stunted. There are those who are spiritually "dwarfed." Their Christian growth doesn't represent their Christian age. I know that maturity is a continual process. I also know that many of us stepped out in areas of ministry less mature than we sometimes wish we had. But, the point is, we continued to allow God to mature us. The problem occurs when a person stops showing growth in his Christian life.

A person without maturity acts like a child; they whine, and cry, and want to be pampered, and have to be continually cared for. Paul talks about the limitations that are imposed when a person's Christian maturity is at this level (Gal. 4). Although he should have authority over many things, he has to defer the administration of these things to someone else. A person cannot accomplish what God is calling him to do in his ministry without maturity.

Another thing about a dwarf is that there is not much chance that they are going to "grow up." Many times when we see someone who is dwarfed spiritually, there is not much chance we are going to see a change. A lack of total commitment plays a primary role in this slow development. Unless they make a total commitment at some point in their life, their maturity will never reach the "height" it should. We could be privileged to attend the finest school in the nation, sit under the greatest of teachers, and have access to the most extensive material in the world; yet, if we refused to take the initiative to learn, we would remain at the same level we began. So it is with the Lord. We can be called to the greatest of ministries, led by the most Godly pastor available, hear the most anointed preaching, and learn from the most scholarly. But, if we neglect to pray, refuse to study, and are careless in our seeking a relationship with the Lord, we will not have the maturity necessary to responsibly carry out our office. God will not increase someone's responsibilities if that person has not proved mature enough to carry out the last responsibilities that He gave them.

9. Blemish in the eye: A person with impaired spiritual sight; they see things in the natural. Jesus spoke of a person who wanted to remove a small object from the eye of another, yet had a large object obstructing his own view (Matt. 7:3-5). This teaching about being judgmental is more than applicable here.

But, let me throw another ingredient into the pot. One of the most frustrating things that I have had to deal with as a pastor is people wanting me to immediately solve a problem they had seen, and yet they had no spiritual insight into that problem. They had observed some of the symptoms and thought they had diagnosed exactly how the problem needed to be dealt with. The Lord had already made me aware of the problem, and I had been seeking the Lord about the timing and the correction. The only reason I had not tended to it already was because He had not allowed me to. In my praying and waiting I had also seen that the root cause was somewhat removed from the visible symptoms, and had some serious spiritual problems associated with it. The person who had come to me demanding a solution, had only seen the obvious and had no clue as to what was really going on. I was not at liberty to fill him in with what the Lord had helped me to see, so now, I had to not only deal with the original person and problem, I had to deal with this other person's impatience and impaired spiritual sight.

There are many things that have to be spiritually discerned (I Cor. 2:14). Although we can not get in the habit of ignoring logistics in dealing with issues, we need to understand there are going to be times when logistics just aren't enough. We need to hear from the Lord on the matter. When God speaks something to our heart we may look at all the logistics and never see how things are going to add up. But, He wants us to be able to step out on faith. When we can do that, and see things happen that cannot possibly take place, then we know it is because He did it, not us.

God will drop into your heart the things you need to see... listen for the thud!

10.Scurvy or scabbed: A person who is ill as a result of a sun deficiency. Sometimes even the most committed can find themselves in a place where they have allowed themselves to have a Son deficiency. We have to guard against our fast paced schedule becoming so crowded we lose time to get alone with God. We must continually pray and seek a relationship with Him.

If the total amount of sun we allowed ourselves to be exposed to was about 5 or 6 hours a week, we could not maintain our health. If the total amount of Son we allow ourselves to be exposed to is about the same, Sunday morning, Sunday night, and Wednesday evening, we will have trouble staying spiritually healthy. Get some exposure!

11. Hath his stones broken: A person who is unable to reproduce. In God's work, it is the person who cannot birth a new Christian into the Kingdom. What good has our teaching or preaching done, if it never accomplishes showing people what it is to be "born again?"

Purposes for Ministry.

Paul wrote to the church at Ephesus, listing in chapter 4 a list of ministries normally referred to as the five-fold ministry (Eph. 4:11). In the verses following this he defines the purposes behind these ministries. In chapter 4 of this book we will explain that ministries will fall under this list, or the ministries of supportive gifts listed in Romans 12:6-8. I do not think that we would be doing harm to say that all ministries should have these purposes as goals.

And he gave some, apostles; and some, prophets; and some, evangelists; and some, pastors and teachers; - Eph 4:11

1. For the equipping (perfecting) of the saints (vs. 12). The Greek word for perfecting actually translates "complete furnishing." God's Word contains everything necessary for a Christian to be equipped to lead a successful victorious walk. But, tools are ineffective if left in the tool chest. God's Word cannot be effective if it is not presented. God chose to minister the presentation of that Word through the agents of ministry listed in verse 11.

2. For the work of the ministry (vs. 12). The ministry that He has placed in us should be a part of the ministry of the local body and a part of the entire ministry of His Church, working together in harmony to promote the Gospel. As I stated earlier, the work of the ministry will be much more effective if it is structured and disciplined. The offices of ministry are part of that structure.

3. For the edification of the body of Christ (vs. 12). The work of ministering should bring us to this goal: the edifying or building up of the Church. I have already mentioned the necessity of one ministry building on the accomplishments of another. But if the whole picture is not one of building up, it has to be one of tearing down, or one that is stagnant. Neither of these will be acceptable to God.

4. For unity (vs. 13 & 16). We talked about unity when we defined teamwork. This unity should be the glue that binds everything together. We should be able to get along so well, each supplying our part, that if one is missing the entire body feels the effect. Properly structured leadership will promote communication and support unity.

5. For maturity (a perfect man) (vs. 13). Here we are talking about maturity again. Verse 14 says that we are not to remain children. There is no better formula for growth in the Lord than to allow His Word to be ministered effectively to us.

6. To allow the fullness of Christ in the Church and us (vs. 13). Again we talk about maturity, but now we add the benchmark. Our goal is to allow the personality of Christ to be in us, bringing us to the standard of perfection that we can only obtain through Him. Effective ministry will teach us the necessary principles to bring this about.

7. For solidness (vs. 14). The Word of God, when ministered, will bring us stability. We will not fall for every doctrine that "blows" through, if we weigh it against His Word, especially if we have others to glean counsel and support from. Ministry encompasses not only the presentation of the Word, but the nurturing of those who receive it. When such a foundation is laid in the lives of those who are involved, solidness or stability is a by-product.

Principles of Leadership.

We have been covering leadership principles from the very beginning of this chapter. But, there are 7 fundamentals of leadership that the Lord put on my heart. I will refer to them as Principles of Leadership.

I need to talk about each of them in turn. But I want to emphasize that they are not listed in any special order, certainly not listed in order of importance. Since they are fundamentals, or principles, they will certainly interface with some of the things that we have already covered, and with some things that we will deal with further along in this book. I will try not to be too repetitious.

1. A Leader must carry Responsibilities.

If we understand our calling to leadership, then we already have a beginning of understanding the responsibility of our ministry. I hope we never lose our enthusiasm or our excitement about what we are called to do. But we need to come to the place where we get the "stars" out of our eyes and face the soberness of the responsibility He has placed with that calling. It is not all going to be fun and games.

We will be inconvenienced. The telephone is going to ring just as we sit down to our meal. Someone will call just about the time we lay our heads on our pillow. Another will want us to pray. We will have to come in from the yard on a Saturday, clean up, put on fresh clothes, and go take care of a need. There will be times of hardship. There will be times of testing. We need to understand that being a leader will cost us. Are we willing to pay the price? I like what Bro. Don Krider (Director of World Wide Ministries, Fresno Ca.) said, "It costs little to put your name on a leadership list; it will cost you everything to be a leader."

Sometimes it is easy to desire the rights, privileges, or even the spotlight of being a leader, but it is something else to be able to accept the responsibilities that go along with them. A calling is not just something placed "on" you, it is something placed "in" you. In fact, when a person has the right spirit about his calling, the rights, the privileges, and especially the spotlight, will be diminished by the satisfaction he receives in just accomplishing what he is called to do. I really believe we have an "acid test" in God's Word of whether we really understand the

63

responsibility of our calling. That is, we must come to the *"Gethsemane"* of our calling. In the Garden of Gethsemane Jesus prayed to the Father, looking ahead at the responsibility of the cross, "O my Father, if it is possible, let this cup pass from me: nevertheless not as I will, but as You will" (Paraphrased from Matt. 26). When we so clearly see the responsibility of the ministry we are called into that we say, "God, I'd rather not have to go through with this because the commitment is so great. However, I do not want my desire to be done, but rather Yours. I will do it for You," we will fully understand our calling.

2. A Leader needs Teaching.

One of the most interesting phrases in Scripture is found in I Corinthians 11:23. To quote Paul, *"For I received of the Lord that which also I delivered unto you..."* It makes me realize that no person can give something that he has not received. I may desire to give one million dollars to you to help in the ministry. I could even tell you that I was going to do it. But, unless I had some-where, somehow received that kind of money, I would not be able to deliver on my commitment. A prime example of this is found in II Samuel 18:21-32. Here we see the story of two messengers, two runners -- Ahimaaz and Cushi. Cushi was told to deliver a message that he apparently knew from first-hand experience (vs. 21. *"what you have seen"*). Ahimaaz, eager to run as he was, was not prepared to deliver the message, but being too impatient to wait his turn continued to insist. Joab finally sent him, but the simple fact that he did not take time to give the message to Ahimaaz suggests that Joab may have just allowed him to go to get him out of his way. I almost said here that Ahimaaz was a better runner and outran Cushi, but it may have been that he took a shortcut. Either way, he beat Cushi to the king, but could not deliver the full message. It was not that Ahimaaz was a bad person (vs. 27 "He is a good man..."). It was not that he had no ministry, he was a runner. It was not that he could not deliver a message. He just went out without proper preparation. Since his preparation was limited, so was his message.

A person answering the call to an area of leadership must take care not to repeat the mistake that Ahimaaz made. Most often when a person is called into a new area of ministry, they need to be taught in that area. And there are many different ways that a person can receive this teaching. The Lord may make the way for that person to attend a Bible school or college. Sometimes a person will receive their teaching by working with someone experienced in the area of the ministry they are called to. The point here is not **HOW** a person is taught, but rather that a person **IS** taught. We must never take shortcuts in God's "school" just to get to the graduation podium. James calls it patience:

But let patience have her perfect work, that ye may be perfect and entire, wanting nothing. -James 1:4

Many times experience is a good teacher. Lessons learned first hand tend to be lessons remembered. A person needs to receive the "Book-learning," but there are also a number of other things that he needs to learn. For instance, he will need to learn to administer what he has been taught. He will need to learn how to "flow" with other ministries around him. He will need to learn the leadership principles presented here. Remember this: Practice may not always make perfect, it may make permanent. If we are going to learn from experience (or practice) we need to be sure that we are exposing ourselves to the right things. The best way to do this is under the covering and guidance of spiritual leadership in the local body. The best place for ministries to be honed is there under the watchful eye of a godly shepherd. And this leads us to the next point.

3. A Leader needs Backing and Covering.

We have already mentioned this when we discussed the topic of launching ministries. We discussed how Paul and Barnabas went out with the support of the church at Antioch. Sometimes we refer to this support as the "covering" of a church or the "backing" of a church. It encompasses both support and accountability. Paul and Barnabas knew that they had the

his local church. They will not shepherd him as his local leadership will, but they should be able to "back" him with verbal
support and prayer support. I know that I have gained the confidence and support of several other churches in addition to my
home church. Just knowing they are praying for me, and they
are concerned about my welfare is the most precious encouragement that I can ever own.

Any leader, regardless of position, should seek to have
godly counsel available to him. Then, he needs to make sure that

---

prayers, the support, and the interest of the believers in the
church at Antioch with them.

I cannot over emphasize the importance of the need for this
type of support! NO LEADER SHOULD EVER TRY TO BE
THE "LONER." We have to guard against the Elijah syndrome,
of "I'm doing it by myself" or "I'm the only one out here doing
it." See what he said, "I, even I only remain..." (I Kings 18:22).
This is an interesting thing for him to say considering he had just
had a conversation with Obadiah about a hundred other prophets
who had been hidden in caves (Vs. 13). Maybe he felt justified
in saying it because he thought he was the only one active at the
time. The spotlight was on him. I do not know. But I do know
this. God finally had to get him to a place where he could listen,
and the message was "I have left me seven thousand in Israel, all
the knees which have not bowed unto Baal..." (Vs. 19:18).
Elijah was not alone by God's choice.

Primarily the source for this backing and support comes from
the local body. Every person should belong to a church, and that
church should support his or her ministry. Even though financial
support may be a part of the church's involvement, it is not the
focus of my discussion here. I am talking about the pastor and
the leadership team recognizing the validity of a person's ministry, being able to endorse that ministry, and feeling they have a
relationship with that ministry. I am talking about the support of
that endorsement, a support that includes prayer, encouragement,
a shoulder to lean on, and someone at your side.

Barnabas deferred a problem to the council of elders at Jerusalem (decision about Greeks needing to be circumcised. Acts 15). Not only did they receive solid godly counsel and a decision; they received support in the communicating of that message to the people. The result was great rejoicing and strengthening of the church. Compare this to the story found in I Kings chapter 12, the story of Rehoboam. This king had wise, seasoned counsel available to him. Yet, his decision not to use this counsel led to the division of the kingdom and his demise. We need to pay attention to what the writer of the scripture in Proverbs has to say about counsel:

> *Where no counsel is, the people fall: but in the multitude of counselors there is safety. -Prov 11:14*

Before I leave this subject, let me point out one last thing. A pastor needs to draw much of this counsel and support from his leadership team. It should be okay for a pastor to be vulnerable and transparent, in front of his leaders. He should develop such a relationship with them that, using wisdom, he could share his needs and/or problems with them. There should be an atmosphere of "no masks worn" as he works with them. This relationship should be built on a foundation of love and honesty between the team and the pastor. It will be harder for the leadership team to support the pastor if he holds them at arm's length and limits the closeness of the relationship.

4. A Leader must Meet Qualifications.

A person who is called to an area of ministry must meet the qualifications for that office before being placed in that office, and must continue to meet those qualifications as long as he fills it. We will discuss the qualifications for each office of ministry in the next two chapters.

5. A Leader must Demonstrate Proper Characteristics.

There are certain characteristics that a leader must possess. These will be covered in detail in the next section of this chapter.

6. A Leader must have Proper Attitude.

There is so much that needs to be said about attitude, and yet I feel that there are scriptures that say everything for me. Let me start with a quote from the Apostle Paul. (I purposely included his title here to remind us of the stature of this man.)

> *For I am the least of the apostles, that am not meet to be called an apostle, because I persecuted the church of God. But by the grace of God I am what I am: and his grace which was bestowed upon me was not in vain; but I labored more abundantly than they all: yet not I, but the grace of God which was with me. -I Cor. 15:9,10*

Can you see the heart of this man! "I'm not even worthy to be an apostle. Because God was so gracious as to call me, I worked as hard as I could. Yet, even my being able to work so hard was because of His grace." God wants men whom, when successful, will give all the glory and honor for that success to Him. He was able to allow such success in Paul's ministry because He knew that Paul would display the proper attitude in his accomplishments.

Jesus commented on this same subject.

> *And whosoever will be chief among you, let him be your servant: Even as the Son of man came not to be ministered unto, but to minister, and to give his life a ransom for many. -Mat. 20:27-28*

68

He also taught a parable against place seeking or self-promotion (Luke 14:7-11) ending His story with this statement.

For whosoever exalteth himself shall be abased; and he that humbleth himself shall be exalted. -Luke 14:11

David displayed this attitude as well. Think about this. This young man was chosen by God to be the next king of Israel (I Sam. 16:12). He was then anointed king before all of those assembled, including his own family (I Sam. 16:13). He then became King Saul's armor bearer, an opportunity that allowed him to live in palace royalty and favor of the king (I Sam. 16:21). But, this young man did not become arrogant or demanding. Instead, when it became necessary, he returned to the wilderness to be a sheepherder. Here he remained until it was God's time to bring him forward again (I Sam. 17:15).

David also knew that when we are successful in accomplishing anything for God that it is God who does it, not us. He was so sure of this that he declared it as he stood before King Saul.

*David said moreover, The **LORD** that delivered me out of the paw of the lion, and out of the paw of the bear, **he** will deliver me out of the hand of this Philistine. -I Sam. 17:37*

There were New Testament characters who understood this as well. Peter:

And when Peter saw it, he answered unto the people, Ye men of Israel, why marvel ye at this? or why look ye so earnestly on us, as though by our own power or holiness we had made this man to walk? -Acts 3:12

and Paul:

Not that we are sufficient of ourselves to think any thing as of ourselves; but our sufficiency is of God; -II Cor 3:5

Part of having the proper attitude is the willingness to "start where you are" or "stay where you are put." It goes hand in hand with the principle we see in Zech. 4:10 of not despising the day of small things in our ministry. We need to remember that we did not start out on top, and when we get there we need to be make noise like the horn, cannot be in control like the steering wheel, cannot be seen like the bumper, but it sure does a good job of holding the wheel on at all speeds.

7. A Leader must Retain Integrity.

It is interesting that when I searched my computer topical Bible for *integrity*, I was pointed to the scriptures that held the qualifications for the offices of deacon and elder. It seems that all of the qualifications that the Lord listed will enable a leader to operate with the integrity that he should have to properly fill those offices. What is integrity? It is defined as sound moral character and honesty. Adhering to moral and ethical principles without compromise. It is the ability to stand at the end of your life and ask your peers the same questions that Samuel asked his (I Sam. 12). "Have I stolen? Have I defrauded any man? Have I oppressed any? Did I receive any bribe? Can you find any ought against me?" It is the ability to have returned to you the answer, "NO!"

This does not mean that we will never make a mistake. I do not judge a person so much by the mistake he has made as I do by his attitude to correct that mistake once it is brought to his attention. Although we are not perfect, and will surely make our share of mistakes, we must operate with the same frame of mind that Paul had:

And herein do I exercise myself, to have always a conscience void of offense toward God, and toward men. -Acts 24:16

70

careful not to have an arrogant attitude towards those who are still starting out. There should never be a "clique" of those that have "arrived." Every time I see someone with that attitude I go to God, asking Him to never let me develop such an outlook. It is not Christ-like, and it is a discouragement to others.

I admire Nehemiah. He had the "start where you are" attitude down pat. He started out as cupbearer, progressed to general contractor, and was finally promoted to governor. In each job he was faithful and uncomplaining. He set an example

---

But have renounced the hidden things of dishonesty, not walking in craftiness, nor handling the word of God deceitfully; but by manifestation of the truth commending ourselves to every man's conscience in the sight of God. -II Cor 4:2

Receive us; we have wronged no man, we have corrupted no man, we have defrauded no man. -II Cor 7:2

Providing for honest things, not only in the sight of the Lord, but also in the sight of men. -II Cor 8:21

If we operate under these guidelines we will be able to stand even if someone chose to falsely accuse.

Having your conversation honest among the Gentiles: that, whereas they speak against you as evildoers, they may by your good works, which they shall behold, glorify God in the day of visitation. -I Pet 2:12

In fact, if we study the word *blameless* in the qualifications for the offices of leadership in I Timothy and Titus, we will see the importance placed on this principle. The word does not mean that we operate questionably and then beat the charges brought against us by going to a court or securing testimonies of witnesses. It means that we are to live our lives in such a way that it would be foolish for a person to even suggest that we had done something wrong. Even if a person maliciously brings up a false charge, those who know us could not entertain it.

material dealing with qualifications for offices of elder and deacon. Then I studied God's Word looking for other components of leadership. I found them in Joshua. Here, in this man, were characteristics that portrayed an exemplary leader. So, as I promised you at the beginning of this book, I am bringing the study back to the Book of Joshua, showing you these characteristics to help you understand why I chose to center my leadership example around him.

And let us not confuse these *characteristics* with *qualifications*. The New Testament clearly sets the qualifications for offices within the Church, and we will cover them in the chapter that deals with those offices. But there are certain characteristics that should be operative in every leader's life as well.

As we study these characteristics, I pray a desire will be created in you to see them developed in your lives. They are godly attributes that He has to develop, but we have to make ourselves available to Him for the developing. I am reminded of the word sanctification -- to set ourselves aside to learn from Him how to become more like Him. If we put on these characteristics, we will have done just that, put on more of His nature.

1. A person who loves God.

A leader must be a person who loves being in the presence of the Lord. This is not a put-on, "I want you to think I like being in church" attitude. It is a genuine love for being where the anointing of God is. This may be the church (it had better be), but it could just as well be that private place that you have established where you can be alone in the presence of God.

This desire is seen in Joshua's life. We have to look closely to see it because it is one of those nuggets hidden away in scripture that can be easily overlooked. In fact, the first time I really paid attention to this scripture, I had to read the text several times to really understand what was being said. Let me set the scene. Moses has made six of the seven trips up Mt. Sinai, where he has received instructions for the nation of Israel. He has set the tabernacle outside the camp and the presence of God in the form of a "cloudy pillar" came and stood at the door. God talked to Moses "face to face" and as the people saw this, they worshipped the Lord. Can you picture this? Moses in the Tabernacle, God on the scene, all of Israel worshipping! But look at this verse:

> *And the LORD spake unto Moses face to face, as a man speaketh unto his friend. And he turned again into the camp:* <u>*but his servant Joshua, the son of Nun, a young man, departed not out of the tabernacle.*</u> *-Ex. 33:11*

Why did God inspire the writer of this Book to include this sentence? He wanted us to see that at a young age, this man who would eventually lead the nation loved being in the presence of God so much that even when Moses went back to the camp, he lingered where God's presence was manifested! It seems Joshua just could not leave as long as there was an opportunity for him to be close to God.

We have the greatest invitation of any dispensation. We are invited to enter into the very throne-room of God. (Heb. 4:16) I have asked the congregation how they would feel if they knew that each of them would have the opportunity, one by one, in the next few hours, to go into the pastor's study and meet Jesus in person. What would they say? How would they make their entrance? I then reminded them that every time they steal away in prayer they are doing just that -- coming into the very presence of God.

Do we desire to be in His presence? Do we value His anointing? Do we love Him with such a love that we long to be very personal with Him? I pray so! Joshua did!

2. A person who trusts God.

Do we trust God? I believe that part of trusting Him is to be able to keep our eyes on Him instead of the overwhelming odds that we are facing. Joshua chose to do this at an early stage in the game. In the 14th chapter of Numbers twelve men stand before the nation and make declaration of their convictions concerning entering the land of Canaan. Ten men, more than the majority, insisted they could not take the land because of circumstances. They had seen themselves as helpless as "grasshoppers" and assumed the giants of the land saw them the same. Two men however, Joshua and Caleb, held another opinion. They encouraged the people with a good report, showing them the fruit the land could produce. Their position was "If the Lord delight in us, then He will bring us into this land, and give it us..." (Num. 14:8).

How could they take such a stand? They had seen giants as well as the other ten. Not only did they have to stand in the face of enemies who were giants, they had to then stand in the face of an entire nation (their peers) that differed with them. I believe they could do so because they remembered what God had already said about the matter and chose to take Him at His word.

I will send my fear before thee, and will destroy all the people to whom thou shalt come, and I will make all thine enemies turn their backs unto thee. And I will send hornets before thee, which shall drive out the Hivite, the Canaanite, and the Hittite, from before thee. - Ex. 23:27,28

Every person in that camp had the same two choices. They could look at the giants, at the awful report of the ten, at the expanse of the land, at the unknowns. Or, they could turn towards the Tabernacle located in the center of the camp, and see the presence of God. It was there, manifested in the form of a cloud for all to see. How could they not trust God with His presence so close? How do we so often fail to trust Him with His presence in our lives?

A leader must learn to trust God for what He says and step out in faith to see His will accomplished.

3. A person who has experienced God's ways.

This speaks of maturity. Yes, I know that we continually grow and mature in our relationship with the Lord, and that our experiencing His way in our lives never ends. But I believe that a person profits by having some experience "under his belt" even as he steps into a leadership role. What things had Joshua seen? Let us take a look:

- Joshua had already seen how God delivered the nation of Israel out of Pharaoh's hand with plagues, yet kept them exempt from these same plagues (Ex. 7-12).
- Joshua had already seen God part the Red Sea for Israel's safe passage, and then drown the best of Pharaoh's army in the same waters (Ex. 14).
- Joshua had already experienced every miracle that God had performed for Israel in the wilderness (Ex. 15-40).
- He saw God deliver the Amalekites, a warring nation, into Israel's hands, a nation not even prepared to do battle (Ex. 17).

He had seen all of these things before he even became the leader of the nation. As leader he then saw:

- The Jordan River parted to allow passage (Joshua 3).
- The Captain of the Host of God near Jericho (Joshua 5).
- The walls of Jericho fall under the shouts and praise of God's people (Joshua 6).
- The sun stand still for almost an entire day (Joshua 10).

As we experience God and see Him faithful to bring us through experiences, it builds our trust, our faith that He can bring us through others. It brings us to the place where we can trust Him quicker and with greater assurance. It matures us.

4. A person who leads by hearing God.

We have already talked about the importance of hearing God, of being Spirit led, and of leading by the directions received from God. Paul was our example of this. (see *Wait on Time and Direction*) Moses was another. God led him back to Egypt, God led him through the plagues, and then God led him to bring Israel out. We see this same ability displayed by Joshua as he takes over after Moses is gone. When God spoke, Joshua simply carried out the orders.

God said to arise and go over Jordan into Canaan. Joshua ordered the leaders:

Now after the death of Moses the servant of the [LORD] it came to pass, that the [LORD spake] unto [Joshua] the son of Nun, Moses' minister, saying, -- Moses my servant is dead; now therefore arise, go over this Jordan, thou, and all this people, unto the land which I do give to them, <even> to the children of Israel. -- Every place that the sole of your foot shall tread upon, that have I given unto you, as I said unto Moses. -- Then Joshua commanded the officers of the people, saying... - Joshua 1:1-3, 10

God said that the Amorites would be defeated despite the fact that they outnumbered Israel. Joshua went into battle:

And the LORD said unto Joshua, Fear them (Amorites) not: for I have delivered them into thine hand; there shall not a man of them stand before thee. --And the LORD discomfited them before Israel, and slew them with a great slaughter at Gibeon, and chased them along the way that goeth up to Bethhoron, and smote them to Azekah, and unto Makkedah. -- And it came to pass, as they fled from before Israel, <and> were in the going down to Bethhoron, that the LORD cast down great stones from heaven upon them unto Azekah, and they died: <they were> more which died with hailstones than <they> whom the children of Israel slew with the sword. - Joshua 10:8, 10, 11

Joshua was sure that he had heard God's directions to defeat the enemy. So sure that he spoke to God about the problem of running out of daylight to fight in. I believe God gave Joshua instructions to command the sun to stand still, and then He honored it:

Then spake Joshua to the LORD in the day when the LORD delivered up the Amorites before the children of Israel, and he said in the sight of Israel, Sun, stand thou still upon Gibeon; and thou, Moon, in the valley of

Ajalon. And the sun stood still, and the moon stayed,
until the people had avenged themselves upon their
enemies. <Is> not this written in the book of Jasher? So
the sun stood still in the midst of heaven, and hasted not
to go down about a whole day. -Joshua 10:12-13

Do we hear God? I believe that He is saying to us what He said to the churches addressed in the Book of Revelation, "He that hath an ear, let him hear." If we are going to lead, we must hear, or else, we are leading on our own!

5. A person who shoulders responsibility.

The first time we see Joshua, Moses sends him to fight (Ex. 17). He did not grumble about how terrible fighting was. He did not argue that they had limited weapons and no experience. He did not fuss about his unprepared army. He did not whine about the danger. He did not complain that Moses was going to be sitting on a hillside watching the fight. He simply did what he was told to do. He shouldered the responsibility of choosing out fighting men and <u>leading</u> them into battle.

Joshua was not afraid to take a stand. We just saw how he stood with Caleb against the rest of the nation's hesitancy to go into Canaan (Numbers 14). There is another instance of his taking responsibility.

...but as for me and my house, we will serve the LORD.
-Joshua 24:15

A leader's responsibility should begin at home and then extend into areas of his office. Demonstrated here, Joshua took responsibility for his own house. He and his family were going to serve the Lord even if they were alone in doing it. But, he felt the responsibility as the leader of the nation to challenge them! His "choose ye this day" was a "put up or shut up." He was responsible to bring the nation to a decision!

There are privileges that come with being a leader. But privilege brings responsibility as well. This blends with *"A Leader must carry Responsibilities,"* a topic that we have previously covered.

6. A person who can be an example.

A LEADER MUST BE **THE** EXAMPLE TO HIS LEAD-
ERSHIP BODY AND TO THOSE AROUND HIM. I have
always marveled at the statement that the Apostle Paul made to
the church at Thessalonica:

> ...but to make ourselves an ensample unto you to follow
> us. -II Thes. 3:9

and to the church at Philippi:

> Brethren, be followers together of me, and mark them
> which walk so as ye have us for an ensample. - Phil 3:17

> Those things, which ye have both learned, and received,
> and heard, and seen in me, do: and the God of peace
> shall be with you. -Phil 4:9

Listen to what Paul is saying! He is asking others to look at
him for an example of how to live a godly life. Could we
encourage a person who had just given his life to the Lord to
look at our walk for an example of how a Christian should act?
Could we as a leader encourage a person freshly called to leadership to mold himself after our example? I believe that every
person should live in such a manner that he or she could be used
as an example, but I also believe the responsibility is magnified
in the life of a leader. Whether he desires it or not, a leader is
going to draw some attention to himself. He will be in the spotlight more and more as he progresses in his life of leading
others. There will always be those who are looking at his life to
learn, and those who are looking to criticize. Because he is put
on such display, he must guard his witness and cultivate these
characteristics.

*I suppose that many of us have wondered if we really are
making a difference for the Lord. I have.

*I was in a Sunday morning service in a church where I
was filling is as interim. Just before I was to step into the pulpit,
the person taking care of the preliminaries allowed a young
man to stand and give a testimony. I had married this young
man and his wife but they lived some distance away and it had

78

been a while since I had seen them. This couple had driven 4 1/2 to 5 hours to be in service there because they knew I was going to minister.

*Let me paraphrase what this young man said as he stood, " I want to say how much I appreciate Bro. Dennis. He doesn't know this, but as a young teenager I saw him at a youth rally, and as he talked that night, he made such an impression on me that I decided to dedicate my life to the Lord and to grow up to be just like him."

*Needless to say tears blur my eyes as I write this just as they did that morning as I listened to this testimony. I had no idea that someone had looked at my life to make a decision to live for God. I wonder if there have been others?

Was Joshua successful at leading by example? It is recorded that he was so successful as a leader that Israel served the Lord as long as he lived, and as long as the leaders he had under him lived.

And Israel served the LORD all the days of Joshua, and all the days of the elders that overlived Joshua, and which had known all the works of the LORD, that he had done for Israel. -Joshua 24:31

Think about this! How would you like to be so successful as a leader that the people you influence will serve the Lord as long as any leader you taught is alive?! I do not believe you accomplish this by telling someone how to live; you accomplish this by showing them how to live.

7. A person with a compassionate heart.

Not every leader will be called to pastor. Yet, every leader must have the same kind of compassion for the people he leads as a pastor does for his congregation. We must literally be willing to become the advocate. Moses did (Ex. 32:30-34). And so did Joshua. When Israel allowed sin to dominate and faced defeat by the men of Ai, Joshua shows his "pastor's" heart going to God on their behalf.

And the men of Ai smote of them about thirty and six men: for they chased them <from> before the gate <even> unto Shebarim, and smote them in the going down: wherefore the hearts of the people melted, and became as water. And Joshua rent his clothes, and fell to the earth upon his face before the ark of the LORD until the eventide, he and the elders of Israel, and put dust upon their heads. And Joshua said, Alas, O Lord GOD, wherefore hast thou at all brought this people over Jordan, to deliver us into the hand of the Amorites, to destroy us? Would to God we had been content, and dwelt on the other side Jordan! O Lord, what shall I say, when Israel turneth their backs before their enemies! For the Canaanites and all the inhabitants of the land shall hear <of it>, and shall environ us round, and cut off our name from the earth: and what wilt thou do unto thy great name? -Josh 7:5-9

A love for the people placed under your care grows as does your relationship with them. But, we have already stated that there is a compassion, a love, and a burden birthed into a leader's heart for his people. Look back at what we discussed under *Pastor must be God Placed.* A pastor should come equipped with a "shepherds heart."

Interactions of Leaders.

My work in the secular world is that of a computer Programmer/Analyst, and one of my primary jobs is to write software for projects. One of the things that I have always had the hardest time with is naming the fields, the files, etc. Well, I guess it has carried over into this book because, for the life of me, I could not think of a better title for this section. I want to deal with the relationship of the leader both to those under his authority and to those to whom he has over him as his leaders. A good leader must recognize that this road travels both ways. Allow me to divide this section into three different areas as I discuss it.

Responsibilities to those under his care.

We have already said that a leader shoulders many responsibilities. One of the greatest of these responsibilities is for that leader to place other ministries, delegate their responsibilities, instruct them in how to carry out these responsibilities, and then encourage them as they do so. This responsibility most definitely applies to the senior pastor as he shapes his leadership team, but is also applicable to any leader who might have a supervisory role over other leaders. I recognize that not all leaders will be in a position to have other leaders assigned to their care, but, even these leaders should develop these skills, readying themselves for the day they might be promoted to a supervisory role. At any rate, all leaders will have someone under their care, and they should understand how to instruct, encourage, and honor these people. In fact, the scriptures make it very clear that God expects a leader to be held responsible for watching over others, and that He will hold them accountable for how they do this.

> *Obey them that have the rule over you, and submit yourselves: for they watch for your souls, **as they that must give account**, that they may do it with joy, and not with grief: for that is unprofitable for you. -Heb 13:17*

I cannot however, cover this topic without saying some specific things about the pastor. His role is unique of all leadership roles in the church since he is the head over all the leadership. God expects him to nurture those ministries He has placed under his care. Paul puts this in perspective for us:

> *Wherefore I put thee in remembrance that thou stir up the gift of God, which is in thee by the putting on of my hands. -II Tim 1:6*

God had given the gift of ministry to Timothy, who was becoming quite a pastor at a young age. Paul as his elder reminded him of the gift, but Timothy had to stir it up, or put it to use. I think that the same principle applied in the church would be something like this: God *gives, the pastor reminds, and the leader stirs.* The gifts and talents in the leader's life are God placed. The pastor focuses attention on these gifts, encouraging their use. With this encouragement, the leader makes full use of them. Paul also stated that when God gave the gift, it was imparted by Paul's laying on of hands. I believe that when God imparts gifts of ministry the pastor should play a role in seeing the leader recognize the imparting of those gifts. He then plays a part in seeing those gifts cultivated.

Paul had another piece of advice for Pastor Timothy:

And the things that thou hast heard of me among many witnesses, the same commit thou to faithful men, who shall be able to teach others also. -II Tim 2:2

Basically Paul was saying this: I did everything in the face of many witnesses, being careful to not do everything myself or alone. I encourage you as a young pastor, Timothy, to not try to do everything that you see needs to be done in your church by yourself. As God shows you faithful men who are called to be leaders, commit the work to them. They in turn will be able to share the load, even teach others.

There are four things that a leader must be able to do to be successful in committing others to areas of leadership. I cannot overemphasize the importance of a leader, especially a pastor, in developing these skills. Pastor, write these down on a piece of paper and post it where it can serve as a reminder. Put it in your Bible. Use it as a checklist from time to time. As long as you are a leader, you should continually carry out these four principles.

1. Recognize them. A leader (especially a pastor) *must* be continually open, allowing God to let him see potential leaders. He must constantly be aware of God's bringing others under him to the place where He wants to set them into leadership areas. In fact, he should be able to help the person being called to recognize what God is doing in his life, giving confirmation, guidance, training, and encouragement to him. This was what Paul was telling Timothy to do when he said to commit the gift of ministry to faithful men.

Moses had this ability. We see it demonstrated the first time that Joshua is mentioned in the scriptures. Joshua was no leader at this time. It would be over 40 years before Joshua would become Israel's leader. Yet, Moses saw a potential captain of an army in Joshua. A captain who would be able to choose men and lead them into battle. A captain who could be trusted and some day molded into a great leader.

And Moses said unto Joshua, Choose us out men, and go out, fight with Amalek: to morrow I will stand on the top of the hill with the rod of God in mine hand. - Exodus 17:9

Moses again shows his willingness to recognize the abilities of men around him, when he becomes aware of a need for someone very knowledgeable in traveling and camping in the wilderness. He sees that someone in his brother-in-law, Hobab.

And Moses said unto Hobab, the son of Raguel the Midianite, Moses' father in law, We are journeying unto the place of which the LORD said, I will give it you: come thou with us, and we will do thee good: for the LORD hath spoken good concerning Israel. And he said unto him, I will not go; but I will depart to mine own land, and to my kindred. And he said, Leave us not, I pray thee; forasmuch as thou knowest how we are to encamp in the wilderness, and thou mayest be to us instead of eyes. And it shall be, if thou go with us, yea, it shall be, that what goodness the LORD shall do unto us, the same will we do unto thee. -Num. 10:29-31

I wonder how many Joshuas and Hobabs have gone unrecognized in our churches because the pastors were so busy doing everything themselves they weren't aware of the help that God wanted to raise up under them? How many men and women have never reached their potential because they became discouraged when they were trying to get started? As leaders, let us pray that God will always cause our hearts to be open to His direction in recognizing and establishing leaders.

2. Honor them and promote them. No leader should be left in the position of having to promote themselves. Whether a ministry is just being started, or an established ministry is changing direction, it needs someone who can promote it. I know, I know... God can promote. And He will. But God's plan is for *every* ministry to be under a leader, and for promotion to come from that leader, keeping that person from having to promote himself. This will remove the danger of that person falling into the area that Jesus taught against in the parable of the ambitious guest (Luke 14:7-14), the danger of a person promoting himself and then having to be removed from his place. Even if a person in ministry has to grow without promotion from someone over him (his leader hasn't learned this principle), he should always guard against place seeking.

God spoke this very clearly to me in my ministry. He called me to be an associate pastor. Until He leads me into another area of ministry, I must remain where I am. I have had to pass up the temptation of stepping into a senior pastor role, even at the encouragement of others, simply because God had not led me there. As I said earlier in this book, sometimes others do not understand. But, until God leads me into a different level or area of ministry, I cannot promote myself to that ministry. God warned me very clearly that doing so would place me outside His calling on my life.

This principle held true even with the writing of this book and the ministry of this material. I went to my pastor when God began to deal with me about the book. I explained what God was leading me to do and asked not only for his support but also for his promotion. Everything I have done in this ministry has been done just that way. Pastor Bob has stood with me, encouraged me, and recommended my ministry in this area to others. Because my pastor is standing with me, so are the other leadership and the congregation of our church. I cannot express the strength and comfort that support has given me.

Let me go one step further here. Moses saw the potential in Joshua, but it was God's command to put his (Moses') honor on Joshua.

And the LORD said unto Moses, Take thee Joshua
the son of Nun, a man in whom <is> the spirit, and
lay thine hand upon him; -- And set him before
Eleazar the priest, and before all the congregation;
and give him a charge in their sight. -- And thou
shalt put <some> of thine honour upon him, that all
the congregation of the children of Israel may be
obedient. -Numbers 27:18-20

As Moses laid his hand on Joshua and declared that he recognized God's calling on him, he was saying to the nation, "You have had trust in me as your leader. I would not recommend someone to you unless I could stand behind him. Trust me and accept this man to lead you as you would accept me."

A good example of this in modern times would be a pastor recommending a ministry to another pastor. Leader, guard your recommendations. Do not give them lightly. But when you see a ministry you can support, especially one under your care, give honor to it by way of recommendation. Put your stamp of approval on it. Attach your name to it in way of reference. (It is okay to give flowers as long as we realize that God supplied the flowers.)

Now take your thumb off them. Guard against smothering those ministries that God wants to grow under you. It is sometimes hard to see someone who comes up in your ranks go into a ministry that may seem to be greater, more dynamic, better known than yours. But a leader cannot limit others to his own accomplishments. **A work limited to one person will never grow beyond that person's capabilities.** Remember this: You may only raise up one, or two, but that one or two could raise up thousands. You may not have the expertise to administer a particular area of need in your church, but someone under you may.

Moses asked God to set someone in as leader of Israel, someone to take the nation into the promised land, knowing that he would not be able to go himself (Num. 27:15-17). Moses promoted Joshua knowing that Joshua would take the nation into greater victories than he had ever been able to do.

I have seen pastors who would not raise up leaders in the church because they had been hurt by someone they had promoted before. Sadly, these kinds of hurts have happened, and will happen again. But this does not annul God's demand for leaders to promote leaders. Jesus spent his entire ministry cultivating leaders. He taught them and nurtured them. He put everything he had into developing their leadership abilities. And he did this knowing that one of them would betray him.

3. Support them. This is a different area than promotion. It deals with supporting the delegated authority of a leader under you. If you delegate responsibility to someone, then never, never circumvent or undermine his authority. To do so tears down the esteem of a leader, and destroys the very nature of leadership structure. IF you feel a different direction needs to be taken, or something needs to be done differently, then go to that leader in charge and work through him. Although you have the final say, both of you should work together to a solution, and, it may take time and prayer to decide what that solution is. When it is reached, if at all possible, let that leader administer the change with your support. Not only will this protect his honor, it will promote leadership ethics to those around you.

And listen to that leader's ideas. Allow him to explain why he wants to implement a certain strategy. Value his abilities and expertise in the area he has been placed. Be open to change, even if it might not be just like you would do it if you were doing it yourself. If there is still a need for something to be done differently than originally planned, allow the person in charge to come into agreement before proceeding.

In all of my years of ministering as an associate pastor, there has never been a decision where I could not come into agreement with my pastor. Sometimes I had to back away from a change I wanted to implement because I saw my pastor's wisdom in not doing what I had suggested. Sometimes my pastor would ask for time to pray about an idea I had brought to him, and would return later to give permission to proceed. Sometimes we were in immediate agreement. Above all, the two of us working together kept us checked against making hasty decisions, possible mistakes.

While I am on the subject, let me turn the table just a little. Leader, sometimes as God leads you to a different area of ministry, you may give up an area that you have overseen for some time. When this happens take your hands off it. Do not try to run it anymore. Give honor to the one who has taken charge. Be very careful with your comments and your actions in regard to how that person is doing things. Let them know that you are available to help them in any way, but do not force your help on them. Unless they are under your supervision, you have no authority to correct them even if you feel correction is needed. If you go to them with suggestions, be careful that you do not give the impression that you are correcting, or that your way is better than the way they are doing. Resist any temptations to influence anyone under that person's care. And, if a person under their care comes to you with a problem about their administration do not entertain it. Refer the person with the problem to that leader, or the pastor, or both.

4. Correct them. Yes, sometimes there is a need for correction. God set the rules and regulations, and the qualifications, for leaders to operate by. Sometimes a leader must also judge the actions of someone under him by these same guidelines, and, if needed, make the necessary corrections. A leader has the responsibility to uphold the offices under his charge, and sometimes correction is involved in this duty.

Correction must follow Biblical guidelines (Matt. 18:15-17, II Cor. 13:1), and proper ethics should always be used when dealing with the situation. Take every precaution not to embarrass the person being corrected, especially in front of his peers. If needed, seek Godly counsel before taking any action. Correct with love. Correct after much prayer and direction from the Lord. Above all, do it with the goal of seeing the person being more firmly established in their area of ministry.

If left unchecked, wrong behavior could hurt the leader or others involved with them. As a parent corrects a child they love for its own good, so must a leader correct someone under their care. This may be as simple as reminding them of their responsibilities (Paul did Timothy). Sometimes it may require the pointing out of a mistake made unawares, a mistake that needs correcting. Other times it may require harsher action.

No one likes being corrected, so when discipline must be administered it requires a God-like spirit on both the person who is correcting and the person being corrected. If you are correcting, make sure you do so with the proper attitude and demeanor. If you are being corrected make sure your reaction is one the Lord can approve of.

Submit to authority above him.

I am going to cover a subject here that is most definitely not a popular subject, most assuredly not a subject that is promoted in the secular world today. A world of the "do your own thing" and "I don't have to answer to anybody" attitude. **I will not hesitate to say that this is one of the most important principles in this book.** A person who is going to be successful in ministry must learn to place himself under godly care, and then submit to the direction of that person. This is most applicable to a person in leadership submitting to his pastor. Since every leader should be accountable, including a pastor having someone over him as a pastor, the same responsibility is placed on everyone in a leadership role. I must return to a scripture that I have already referenced to point out that we have a directive from God's Word to place ourselves in this kind of accountability.

> *Obey them that have the rule over you, and submit yourselves: for they watch for your souls, as they that must give account, that they may do it with joy, and not with grief: for that is unprofitable for you.* -Heb 13:17

Well, it is easy to see that we have this directive, but what does it really mean? (Sometimes we just need to take a common sense approach to understanding these things.) I do not know of anyone who instantly knew how to be led of the Lord when they first came into relationship with Him. Being led of the Lord is something we learn more and more about as we develop that relationship. Since being Spirit led is something that a person must learn, and this learning curve requires time, there is a great need to have someone who can give Godly direction and counsel during the process. In fact, I would venture to say that we are continually learning to be led of the Lord, no matter how long we have been in the ministry. There will always be the need for us to have someone who can stand with us in prayer, counsel, and support. We seek out people who are knowledgeable in certain subjects to teach us in the secular world. How much more does it make sense to place ourselves under someone knowledgeable in the ways of the Lord to be taught?

I will go so far as to say this. If you are filling a leadership role in the local body, your first responsibility is to show those under your leadership your commitment to your spiritual leader. **Just as the pastor is to be the example of leadership, each leader must be THE example of how to operate under that leadership.** If you are not going to be this example, you have no business being in any role of leadership. YOU CANNOT BE A LEADER IF YOU DO NOT KNOW HOW TO SUBMIT. I like the way Bro. Don Krider said it in his teaching on the spirit of wisdom, "Wisdom gives you a power to submit yourself to authority. If you cannot submit yourself to authority, you will never be a leader."

*I am not teaching something here that I have not lived. I have been in the office of elder, associate pastor, and co-pastor. I have filled the pulpit in my home church and in other churches as guest speaker. God put it in my heart early in my ministry that I had an obligation to submit myself to pastoral authority. I have learned that this type of submission builds trust.

*I will never forget a minister at a conference asking me what my ministry was. When I replied that I was a co-pastor, he pointedly told me that this type of relationship would never last. His inference was that sooner or later two people pastoring together would find unsolvable differences. Well, that was ten *years ago and I am still pastoring with the same man. The reason. I know he is my senior pastor, and I submit myself to his authority without question. If I did not have enough trust in him as my pastor to do so, I would not stay at his church. Since, there is no question about seniority, thus no power struggle, we are both free to have God's direction in the church.*

*In fact, God dropped something into my heart that I have shared with my pastor and our church on several occasions. As long as he and I are standing in agreement there will never be any major church split. Oh, some may come and some may go, but we will never face the kind of split some have faced. There is power "where two or more agree" (Matt. 18:19,20).

So, what does it mean to be submissive? Well, this powerful word, by definition, has two parts, *sub*, meaning under, and *mission*. We each are responsible for a part of, or *sub*-part, of a mission. Even more importantly, we are all involved in the same mission. God just placed us in different areas of responsibility. And, all of these areas have to fit together. (Now we are back to our discussion of teamwork. I told you many of these principles overlapped.) The pastor, under the direction and supervision of the Holy Spirit, coordinates his leadership team to accomplish this.

There is one thing that submission is NOT. Submission is not blindly following someone. If any leader over you should promote anything that does not line up with God's Word, it is error, and you should not follow him into that error. We have seen examples where people blindly follow others into this kind of error, and it has given the principle of submission a black eye. Weigh everything against the Word. If there is error, and that error cannot be brought to light and corrected, then pull away from that leadership, and find leadership that does line up with God's Word.

*Yes, we have seen error. We have even seen those who allowed themselves to get into trouble, and those who would exploit the fact that some did. But my answer has always been this. I can stand and list the names of good, God-fearing, solid men who have not compromised their integrity nor their

lifestyles. And that list is much longer than the list of those who have fallen. Do not go looking at those who have failed. Look to those who carry the torch faithfully.

Submission does mean, however, that you recognize your spiritual leader as being THE person God has placed in that position for your growth, guidance, and safety. Treasure it! Draw from it! Honor it! And do not run off everywhere else getting counsel. I really suspect that something is not in order if a person continually runs to others for counsel, and never goes to their pastor. There is nothing wrong in having others you can confide in, and even receive counsel from, but these others should never replace counsel from your pastor.

Let me wax practical one more time. There will be times as a leader that you will not immediately agree with what your pastor is going to do. Most disagreements come from misunderstanding or miscommunication. Keep the communication channels open. I do not think that there can be such a thing as too much communication. If you find yourself in a situation where you disagree with the pastor about an issue, do it with him!!!! Do not carry it to others for discussion, not even to other leaders. Most of the time, the more a disagreement is talked about, the worse it becomes. Do not procrastinate going to him. Do not harbor it. Go to the pastor immediately before feelings on the subject deepen. Stop only long enough to pray.

But know this. The pastor has the final say. He is the shepherd responsible to God for the sheep under his care, and if at all possible you should support him in his decision even if you do not ever see it exactly the way he does. If the issue is one that you cannot support in any form, be careful of your actions. There is strong language in the Bible on the topic of touching God's anointed ones.

*Most of us who are married will share things with our spouse, and rightly so. I share everything with my wife, things that I could never share with anyone else. Sometimes this means we are discussing things that are of concern between our pastor and us. Many times these topics are ones that are close to my

heart. When I do this, I am careful to make sure the discussion takes place with the right attitude. As we talk of them, I want to be careful that I am not being critical or negative. Prayer for my pastor, for myself, and for the situation seems to be the best way to keep everything adjusted.

Pastor, let me bring this to your attention. If someone comes to you with something that he is in disagreement with, you had better listen, even if that person is angry. If you do not let him vent his disagreement with you, you can bet that he will vent it somewhere else. You have the responsibility of maintaining the communication channels in your leadership team. You also have the responsibility of seeing these matters settled. Pray and get God's direction. Maybe it means moving a little slower in implementing a change, waiting until all are in agreement. Remember this as well, though. You still have the responsibility of not compromising what God has led you to do.

Sadly, there will be those who will not submit to leadership. I could list examples of those who wanted to be in leadership, but could not be placed there because they could not submit to pastoral authority. Most of the time these people will not stay at any one church for any extended period of time. As soon as they realize they have to operate under guidelines they leave. (I have always been amazed at how they suddenly hear the Lord leading them somewhere else.) It has also been my observation that people who cannot submit themselves to pastoral authority usually cannot submit themselves very well to God. Just a while ago I heard a minister declare from the pulpit, "If God can't keep them, pastors, we don't need to. If they won't accept leadership principles we don't need them at all." When I first heard this I thought it was a harsh statement. But when I reflect on the problems that seem to follow these people, I might agree. We need to quit pampering people who refuse to line up with God-given principles. The Bible actually speaks of being delivered, or rescued, from people who will not reasonably line up with godly principles and who are malicious towards ministry. The terminology is "unreasonable and wicked men."

And that we may be delivered from unreasonable and wicked men: for all men have not faith. -II Thes. 3:2

This deliverance will cause the Word to have "free course" and be glorified (II Thes. 3:1).

There is a beautiful illustration of submission in the first chapter of Acts. The disciples had just seen the risen Lord! For forty days he had ministered to them after his resurrection! How anxious they must have been to tell the world about this experience! Then Jesus gave them their instructions. They were to wait in Jerusalem until the promise of the baptism of the Holy Ghost had been fulfilled (Acts 1:4, 5). Wait?! For how long? Can you imagine how hard that might have been with the message of the risen Lord burning within them? But wait they did. And the result was not only the most tremendous event of their lives, it was a tremendous church growth as well.

Paul displays yet another example. In Acts 21:17-26 we see his willingness to submit to the authority of pastor James in Jerusalem. Here he was, an apostle. He had authority. He had direction from God in his life. He had results of an anointed ministry. Yet, Paul went to the pastor and the elders, detailed the activities of his ministry, and then listened to their counsel concerning a Jewish misunderstanding of that ministry. Knowing that he was not bound by the Jewish traditions, he saw the wisdom in their counsel to reach out to the Jews, and agreed to follow certain rituals. Paul was obedient even though it cost him much criticism.

Submitting ourselves to proper authority should bring loyalty in any relationship. We can truly become that "friend that sticketh closer than a brother" (Prov. 18:24). As leaders we should be able to echo the words of Joshua's leadership team:

And they answered Joshua, saying, All that thou commandest us we will do, and whithersoever thou sendest us, we will go. According as we hearkened unto Moses in all things, so will we hearken unto thee: only the LORD thy God be with thee, as he was with Moses. -Josh 1:16,17

Support and uphold the pastor.

I want to narrow the focus for a few minutes, looking at how the leadership team should support the pastor. The team should make a conscious effort to strengthen the pastor, lightening his load so that he is able to focus on the task before him of shepherding the sheep. I was at a Men's Wake-up Call, a local meeting of the Promise Keepers, where I saw a wonderful illustration of men supporting the pastor's load. Each pastor was asked to stand and raise both arms. We all know that holding both arms up for a length of time becomes very tiring. Then, men who were around the pastors were asked to go to them and hold their arms up for them. The pastors were instructed to relax and allow all the weight of their arms to be supported by these men. In this beautiful illustration of support, the men prayed for the pastor whose arms they were holding. While we cannot physically go around holding our pastor's arms, we can spiritually hold them by praying for him and by giving him our support.

There are three areas of support for the pastor that the Lord put in my heart.

1. Prayer support. Prayer support for the pastor means [1.] praying for the pastor and [2.] carrying some of the pastor's burden for the congregation by praying for them. If you are in a position of leadership and you do not daily pray for your pastor and for the congregation of your church, shame on you! (One of my editors commented that this was "pretty strong." I wrestled with removing it, of toning it down, but I decided not to soften the blow. The importance of prayer in the leadership ranks weighs to heavily.) You want your pastor to be successful -- pray for him. You want your pastor to be on fire -- pray for him. You want to see things happen in the church -- pray for him.

2. Voice of approval. Others around you, especially the congregation, will perceive your support of the pastor based on how you talk about him or about the things he is trying to accomplish. Attitude speaks very loudly. The tone of what you say speaks volumes. Your expressions sometime speak louder than words. Take every opportunity to speak in behalf of your pastor. Honor him with your words. Praise him before others!

Many years ago the Lord put in my heart to always honor the pastor whose pulpit I am filling. Most of the time I am filling in while he is gone. From the pulpit, I build him up to his congregation. Then I have the congregation stand with me, and we pray for him. I try to pray specifically that God will bless him, especially on the mission he is on at the time. I do this in every service I minister in. It allows the people to see my support and honor for the man of God that is over them.

I also voice this principle to the congregation of our church. "Do not come to me to complain about the pastor or what he is doing. I will not talk to you. Not alone anyway. I will get you by the arm, and you and I will go directly to the pastor! If it is worth talking about, it is worth doing so in his company. I will not entertain any discussion about him without his presence."

I have maintained this principle since I first filled the role of associate pastor. It is a vital area of integrity that I have maintained for all these years. As yet, I have not had anyone try me. I believe it just circumvents any problem in this area.

Leader, there are many ways to honor your pastor vocally. A positive comment about his ministry, publicly voicing appreciation for his care, telling him and others how you appreciate his solidness as a shepherd... these are all examples. There is one more example that is close to my heart. When addressing your pastor in front of others honor him with a title. Address him as pastor or brother. It's okay to call him by his first name when you are alone, but show your respect for him before others by using a title.

3. Action support. Every action we take as a leader should be one to support and strengthen our pastor. We should strive to aid the pastor in reaching the people. The larger the congregation, the more important it is for this to happen. The pastor is just one person, and one person can only reach so many at a time. In fact, I believe the primary goal of the leadership body, as a whole is this: WE SHOULD PLACE THE HAND OF THE PEOPLE INTO THE HAND OF THE PASTOR. We should be his hands, ears, eyes, and mouth, representing him to the people. We should be able to present the people back to him as well. He should be able to feel the pulse of the people through his leadership team at any time.

Priorities and Relationships.

We have talked considerably in this chapter about leadership. The callings, principles, characteristics, and interactions. I would be amiss if I did not mention that our ministry should be balanced in our lives.

I thank God that I was privileged to sit under teaching by men of God that understood that it was NOT God's intention that a person's ministry be fulfilled at the expense of every thing around him, especially his family. We must balance what we say here, because we know that we cannot approach our calling to ministry frivolously or as a novice. Neither can we let those around us sway us from our ministry. However, if we understand how to prioritize areas in our lives, our ministry will be strengthened rather than neglected. I was privileged some years ago to sit under a comprehensive teaching on relationships and priorities under Dr. Harold Eiland. Here was a man, who I considered to be one of the finest men of integrity and knowledge, telling me that it was not just okay, but was God's will that I prioritize taking care of myself, and my family, and then my ministry.

So impressed was I, that I asked Bro. Eiland for his material and have taught it several times from the pulpit. With his permission I am going to give a brief outline of the principles involved in this teaching. The entire study is quite lengthy so the outline that I am giving here is only a part of Bro. Eiland's outline. I am going to list the relationships that we need to develop, and I am going to list them in the order that they should be prioritized. As leaders it is imperative that we get these in the proper order.

I must develop the relationship of:

1. Me to God.

There are two kinds of relationships - intrapersonal and interpersonal. An intrapersonal relationship occurs when the relationship is somewhat one-sided (like boss to employee). We need to develop a two-sided, interpersonal relationship between God and us, with Him as our number one priority.

But seek ye first the kingdom of God, and his righteousness; and all these things shall be added unto you. -Matt. 6:33

"Sometimes our greatest moments are times when we communicate to God or to other people without words." says Bro. Eiland. Let us develop this closeness with God.

2. Me to Me.

This might sound odd at first, developing a relationship with ourselves. But, we need to move past any complexes that we have about ourselves if we are to minister to others with our full potential. We can dispel our feelings of inferiority or poor self-image when we begin to understand what God thinks of us, and begin to be able to adjust ourselves to His way of thinking about us. Man is: God's created image (Gen. 1:26), God's friend (II Chron. 20:7), the apple of His eye (Psalm 17:8), His child (John 1:12), His heir (Romans 8:14-17), and His purchased possession (I Cor. 6:19-20).

We can improve our self-image if we realize who and what we are according to God's Word,

But as many as received him, to them gave he power to become the sons of God, even to them that believe on His name. -John 1:12

and then begin to think it,

For as he thinketh in his heart, so is he... -Proverbs 23:7

and to speak it.

Death and life are in the power of the tongue... -Proverbs 18:21

97

3. Me to Spouse.

The family is the first and foremost institution in God's eyes. He even chose the family to be representative of the relationship between Jesus and the Church. There are five steps to a good husband / wife relationship:

1. Love. All three types of love (eros, phileo, agape) should be active in a family.

2. Respect. Respect has to be: Earned when on the receiving end. Recognized and given when not on the receiving end. Worked at no matter what end. Neglect will always tear down respect.

3. Communication. We must have intercommunication in our relationship. That is, one talks while the other listens. We listen when we feel the other person has something worthwhile to say.

4. Consideration. Simply do not ask anything of a partner that you would not desire to be asked of you in reverse circumstances.

5. Conciliation. Marriage is not a 50-50 proposition. If you are not giving 100%, then you are not doing your best for the marriage. Be the one to initiate the effort to bring the relationship back together again.

4. Me to Children.

Both parents are responsible to share in the training of the child, but the headship of the home and the ultimate responsibility falls on the husband. Children should be taught and directed: to fear God (Psalms. 34:11), to respect and trust God (Matt. 19:14, Eccl. 12:1), to honor parents (Eph. 6:1-3, Prov. 23:22, Col. 3:20), and to have discipline and respect (Heb. 13:17, Prov. 19:18). It is the parent's responsibility to teach these things, at the same time give correction (Prov. 13:24, 23:13-14), and guard against abuse (Col. 3:21). (There is a "bad roots / bad fruits -- good roots / good fruits" principle. What is allowed to grow in a child will be evidenced in the fruit of their life.)

5. Me to my Job.

God intended for man to work from the very beginning (Gen. 2:8, 15). It was not until the fall of man into sin that work became labor (Gen. 3:17-19). There is a New Testament principle that a man should work and support his family (I Tim. 5:8, II Thess. 3:10). But as we go about the duty of performing our job, we must make sure our gain is acquired in the right manner (Prov. 13:11), and guard against gain becoming a priority that owns us (I Tim. 6:5).

6. Me to my Ministry.

Law of ministry. You can not give what you have not received. We need to study to show ourselves approved (II Tim. 2:15). This entire book builds the tools needed for us to use in our ministry.

7. Me to Others.

We have to be careful that we do not let others, even those in need, demand so much of our time that we neglect all else. The parable of the Good Samaritan illustrates the proper attitudes on the part of the "Samaritan" and the "Ditch Person" (Luke 10:25-37). We could find ourselves in either role from time to time.

Samaritan: 1. Had the right motive. 2. Had Compassion. 3. Had the proper tools to assist.

Ditch Person: 1. Was quiet, not demanding. 2. Was cooperative and obedient. 3. Should show both immediate and long-term improvement.

We see that even in the Old Testament the Lord was concerned with our relationship to others. Six of the Ten Commandments deal with man's relationship to each other. In the qualifications set down for a person to be able to fill a leadership role (elder or deacon) (I Tim. 3:2, 7, 10; Titus 1:7,8) it is clear that God expects a person to have the best rapport in the community and in society that is possible. If a person has poor character with others in his community, his ministry will suffer for it.

In Conclusion.

We have talked at quite length about leadership and leadership roles. In summary let me leave you with:

Exhortation.

Jesus made clear in his teaching on the parable of the talents that he expects a return when he invests in a person. And investments have been made. In a leader He instills talents, callings, and anointing. Peter gives this exhortation:

> *As every man hath received the gift, <even so> minister the same one to another, as good stewards of the manifold grace of God. -- If any man speak, <let him speak> as the oracles of God; if any man minister, <let him do it> as of the ability which God giveth: that God in all things may be glorified through Jesus Christ, to whom be praise and dominion for ever and ever. Amen. -I Pet 4:10, 11*

Paul writes to a close friend and champion of the Gospel:

> *And say to Archippus, Take heed to the ministry which thou hast received in the Lord, that thou fulfil it. - Colossians 4:17*

And then Paul gives this exhortation to a young minister.

> *Preach the word; be instant in season, out of season; reprove, rebuke, exhort with all longsuffering and doctrine. -II Tim 4:2*

Notice of Resource.

Jesus said that He could not do anything without the Father doing it through Him. So, how can we expect to? Our duty is to present ourselves as a vessel for Him to pour into and out of. Our sufficiency is in knowing that we can do all things through Him.

> *Not that we are sufficient of ourselves to think any thing as of ourselves; but our sufficiency <is> of God; Who also hath made us able ministers of the new testament;*

not of the letter, but of the spirit: for the letter killeth, but the spirit giveth life.-II Cor. 3:5-6

The task.

The task of leading is an awesome one, so overwhelming that at times we may wonder if we will be successful in accomplishing what we know God put in our hearts to do. How do we attack such a task? Can we make a difference? Let me leave you with a story I once heard that illustrates an attitude we might develop.

Once, a man walking down a beach saw another man standing next to a tremendous mountain of starfish that had washed ashore. He observed the man methodically casting one after another back into the safety of the sea. "What are you doing?" asked the man. "Saving these starfish." replied the other. "You cannot possibly save all these starfish." the first sarcastically replied, looking at the innumerable mound before them. "I can save this one" replied the other, as he tossed one more back into the sea!

May God undergird you as you toss!

Chapter 3

THE PASTOR

Who is a Pastor?

This is the question I have challenged my audience with at the very beginning of each teaching of this material. I issue a further challenge during the first night of the study, "Find me a scripture in the Bible that says to set into office a man of leadership and give him the title *pastor*." I have found this to be an effective method for provoking discussions on the subject, and I always enjoy the different ideas it generates. There will always be those who come to me puzzled because they cannot seem to put their finger on the particular scripture. Also, when I teach this lesson, I introduce it by asking, "Are you ready to talk about the Pastor?!!!" It is a sure-fired way to grab their attention, and after having done so, I try to answer these questions. Now that I have yours, let me see if I can do the same.

This part of the study actually took me by surprise. I hope you don't mind my being so transparent. I certainly pray that my doing so doesn't cause you to loose confidence in my writing. But, as I began to list the different offices we have in the local church, I discovered a problem I had never thought of before. I could put my finger on scriptures to support elders, deacons, and even the other offices in the church, but for the life of me I couldn't find the "Thus shalt thou do" when it came to placing a pastor. I sheepishly approached several other ministers with the question, hoping all the time that they would not laugh at me and then spread the word of my limited knowledge. But, I was able once again to lift my head when the replies were, "Well, I really haven't thought of it that way." I generated a lot of discussion, and most of the information in this chapter came from research that discussion led to. I began to dig for answers. The way I saw it, we either had to back it up scripturally or dismiss all of the pastors. (Being a pastor myself, I was sure relieved to find that we were scripturally correct!)

We defined in chapter 1 our first element of scriptural structure. In the text in Joshua it was Joshua who emerged as the man God had called to lead the nation of Israel into the promised land. He is the person God set in as the leader. In our New Testament structure we refer to this leader as a *pastor*. Now let's sum these two together and add another fact that we will discuss in this next section to get our description of this office. **A pastor is a leader who has been called and placed by God to shepherd those people placed under his care.** We spent a great deal of time in chapter 2 talking about the leadership role that a person could fill, and every aspect of that leadership role applies to the pastor; he is not exempt. In addition, we will talk about this man in the other chapters of this book, because the pastoral role is one that touches every other leadership area.

Scriptural Support.

A Shepherd.

We find no single scripture in the Bible that simply says to set a man into office and call him by the term pastor. The word *pastor* is the Latin word for *shepherd* and goes back to ancient times, describing those men who would take on the role of *leading* or *overseeing* a *flock* of people. We find the word used in the book of Jeremiah eight times. In these scriptures there is promise,

And I will give you pastors according to mine heart, which shall feed you with knowledge and understanding. - Jer. 3:15

and there is warning.

Woe be unto the pastors that destroy and scatter the sheep of my pasture! saith the LORD. -Jer. 23:1

The usage of the word in Jeremiah is to *tend the flock* but the same Hebrew word (Ra ah) is also translated as "feed" or "ate". We begin to develop a feel for the significance of the title *pastor*. He is to be a person who oversees a congregation, guarding them, caring for them, and feeding them.

The word is found only once in the New Testament, in Ephesians 4:11, where the five-fold ministry is listed.

*And he gave some, apostles; and some, prophets; and some, evangelists; and some, **pastors** and teachers; - Eph 4:11*

The Greek word here is *poimen*, which again means *shepherd*. We can relate this to the term overseer in Acts,

*Take heed therefore unto yourselves, and to all the **flock**, over the which the Holy Ghost hath made you **overseers**, to **feed** the church of God, which he hath purchased with his own blood. -Acts 20:28*

where we find several interesting words in the same passage. First the Greek word for flock is *poimnion*, and is related to the word *poimen*, for *shepherd*, in Ephesians 4:11. The word for overseers is *episkopos* and is defined as a superintendent or officer in charge of a church. And then, the word feed is the Greek word *poimaino* which means *to tend as a shepherd*. This scripture in Acts is actually a charge given by Paul to the <u>leaders</u> at Ephesus, and leaves little doubt that the words are describing the same office or work (see next section "An Elder").

Jesus understood this role. He is referred to as the great shepherd of the sheep (Heb. 13:20), the Good Shepherd (John 10:11,14), the Chief Shepherd (I Peter 5:4). Jesus not only fulfilled the role, He also taught about it with passion:

And Jesus, when he came out, saw much people, and was moved with compassion toward them, because they were as sheep not having a shepherd: and he began to teach them many things. -Mark 6:34

He gave this commandment to Peter, "Feed my sheep" (John 21:16) who later would pen these words,

Feed the flock of God which is among you, taking the oversight thereof, not by constraint, but willingly; not for filthy lucre, but of a ready mind; -I Pet. 5:2

The role of pastor was to quickly become one of the most important roles in the development of the Church. These pastors were not going to be men who moved around, coming and going. Rather, they were to be settled in the church, permanent fixtures that could be busy about the work of the congregation. In fact they were to be the ones who would *rule* over the local body. (I have been told that the word *rule* is translated *pastor* in the Spanish Bible.) This person would always be the one "on point" when moving forward. (We will discuss in a moment the authority of a pastor to do this.) Remember this principle about shepherds. They cannot drive their sheep, but must always lead them.

An Elder.

By now someone who is reading this, and checking the scripture context around the verses that I have used, has made the discovery that these verses have been directed to the elders of the churches. And you might be wondering how this is applicable to the pastor. Well, quite frankly, the pastor is an elder. The terms are synonymous. A pastor must meet every qualification that the scriptures lay down for this office, as well as all of the characteristics of leadership that we have already dealt with. (We will discuss the qualifications of the elders in the next chapter.) A pastor is not exempt because of position or stature. If anything he has more responsibility to maintain these standards because of his example to the people.

We see Peter, an apostle, who begins to operate in an area very much like the role of pastor in the book of Acts, referred to as an elder.

The elders which are among you I exhort, who am also an elder, and a witness of the sufferings of Christ, and also a partaker of the glory that shall be revealed: -I Peter 5:1

We will also see in this next section that there must be one elder that has the mantle of authority. His role will be the lead role, the pastor. As Pastor Dub Williams puts it, he has on him the "badge of authority." The local body, like any body, must have only one head. Since we find no one scripture that commands this, we must study the New Testament to see if there are other scriptures that deal with the subject. When we do, we find a definite pattern emerges that supports it.

A Pattern in Jesus' ministry.

The pattern in scripture supporting a person being the *chief* elder or pastor, and supporting ministry in leadership under him, is first seen in Jesus' ministry. We have already stated that Jesus was the Good Shepherd (John 10:11,14), the Chief Shepherd (I Peter 5:4). We also can see in scripture that Jesus had multitudes of people that followed His ministry, a congregation if you will (Matt. 4:25, 8:1, 12:15, etc.). But, we also see that Jesus chose out seventy to a special role called disciples.

After these things the Lord appointed other [seventy] also, and sent them two and two before his face into every city and place, whither he himself would come. - Luke 10:1

Then, seeing the need for shepherds over the people (Matt. 9:36), Jesus called twelve disciples together, gave them instructions as well as power to minister the Gospel, and commissioned them as apostles.

And when he had called unto <him> his twelve disciples, he gave them power <against> unclean spirits, to cast them out, and to heal all manner of sickness and all manner of disease. -- Now the names of the twelve apostles are these... -Matthew 10:1, 2

Of these twelve men, Jesus seemed to hold three of them (Peter, James, and John) in a different light of ministry than the others. This becomes evident in several events that took place where these were the only men who were allowed to be present.

In the raising from the dead of Jarius' daughter, it is written that Jesus "suffered (allowed) no man to follow him, except Peter, and James, and John the brother of James" (Mark 5:37, Luke 8:51). It seems, by the wording here that there were others who wanted to go, but Jesus allowed only these three. When Jesus went up into the mountain to be transfigured, He allowed only these same three to go with Him (Matt. 17:1,2). Again, these were the only three that went further with Jesus when he came to the Garden of Gethsemane (Matt. 26:37, Mark 14:33) to pray. In fact, many commentaries refer to these three as the "inner circle" of the apostles.

The Gospels, especially John, make it evident too, that John was one of, if not the most prominent of the apostles, and greatly loved by Jesus. So, was Jesus playing favorites? Can He be accused of discriminating? **NO! But Jesus did recognize those ones around Him who could be set into the various positions of leadership.** He knew the seventy who could go and minister. He knew the twelve who would give honor to the call of apostle. He also knew that three showed enough understanding and maturity to be intimately closer to His ministry at the time. It might be suggested that each of the three were given special commissions: Peter was the first to preach to the Gentiles, James the first to be martyred, and John the first (and only) to receive the last revelation of Jesus.

The ministry of Jesus was recorded for an example, and it appears that He wanted leadership to be a part of it. He showed that He knew how to deploy these men in their leadership roles. The story of the feeding of the five thousand serves as a good example (Luke 9). The apostles came to Jesus with a request to allow the people to leave so they could acquire food. Jesus had a different vision; He wanted them fed. As he looked at the crowd which numbered more than 5000, He also knew He would not be able to feed each one personally. He organized the effort, dividing the crowd into groups of 50. Now, instead of 5000 contacts, there were 100. Now instead of each team member having to reach over 400, they could reach 10. He organized the group into a number easily reached by his *team*. He then delegated the disciples to the ministry of distributing the meal to the companies. Because of His wisdom in using the men around Him, the need was met more efficiently.

A pattern in the New Testament Church.

In the recording of the birth and growth of the Church in the New Testament, we continue to see this pattern emerge. (The pattern of a person ministering in an area of overseeing a particular church body. A pastor, if you will.) In Acts 11:19-26 Barnabas is sent to oversee the church at Antioch. Later it is said that he went to the island of Cyprus (Acts 15:36-39), possibly to oversee the church there. Timothy was sent by Paul to help the church at Philippi (Phi. 2:19) and later to pastor the church at Ephesus (I Tim). Titus was sent to the church at Crete (Titus 1). These men were not only to establish the church, but also to help bring the church to maturity, placing others in leadership under them.

The form of organization set in by these apostles, and by the New Testament believers, is thought to have followed the pattern of synagogue worship that was prevalent at the time. The synagogue worship had emerged as the Tabernacle worship ended. (It is interesting to note that God had appointed specific men to specific ministries even in the Tabernacle worship. See Leviticus and Numbers.) The size and the structure of the synagogue varied with the population, but if we look at the worship and the structure, we see some significant similarities to the type of services we have in our churches today. Let us take a quick look.

At the upper end of the building was the ark, a chest in which was placed the Book of the Law. In front of the ark was placed an eight-branched lamp. Toward the center of this upper end of the building was a raised platform on which several persons could stand at once. In the middle of this platform rose a pulpit behind which the reader stood to read the lesson for the service. In towns small in size there would be only one rabbi (priest). If a fuller organization was possible, there was a college of elders (Luke 7:3) presided over by one who was *"ruler"* or *"chief ruler"* of the synagogue (Luke 8:41, 49, 13:14, Acts 18:8, 17). There was a minister of the synagogue called a *"chazzan"* who had duties resembling those of the Christian deacon (Luke 4:20).

The order of the service was this: The Law of Moses was read every Sabbath on a schedule that would allow the whole law to be completed in a three-year cycle. Next, the writings of the prophets were read as a second lesson. These were followed by the *"derash"* or the exposition, the sermon of the synagogue (Acts 13:15).

While our structure today varies somewhat from locale to locale, and while it does not exactly match this pattern of the synagogue, we would have to work at **not** seeing similarities. I am not bringing this pattern to your attention to suggest copying it, or even measuring the accuracy of our structure against it. I merely want to help us understand how our structure *may* have come about, as we look at the facts surrounding a person being set over a congregation as its head. I also want to show that our structure, which has remained fairly consistent over the decades, emerged from the only type of organization and worship these new Christians knew. From the way God has blessed it, one might conclude that He has been pleased.

Office of Pastor.

As you know by now, I said much about the office of pastor when I covered the leadership principles. And, we just discussed the fact that his primary responsibility is to shepherd the sheep. However, I want to make two more areas very clear. These two areas are the pastor's authority and the pastor's voice.

Pastor's authority.

We mentioned in the topic of submission in the previous chapter that one essential area was being submitted to the authority of a pastor. I think we have spent ample time on that subject, but I need to make clear the pastor's authority over the church, and deal with some concerns that giving a person this type of authority might generate.

The pastor has to have authority in the local body, including, of course, the spiritual authority over the congregation and leadership. But, I believe it also includes authority in the corporate structure of the church as well. I know I risk generating some disagreement here, but I feel the pastor should not be under the corporate board's directive, rather, the pastor should be the president of the corporation, placing him in a position of authority over the Board. A pastor should not have to worry about his authority being challenged or undermined by the corporate board, the leadership, or the congregation. He should not have to concern himself about being dismissed by the Board, or having to pass a periodic vote by his congregation. He should be free to lead as the Spirit of the Lord directs, with the backing of his authority by all these parties. Because of this, he must exercise full leadership over all the offices of the local church, and this includes the Board of Directors. (This encompasses the chairing of any and all meetings that the Board might have. No meeting should take place in the church without the pastor's knowledge and approval.)

Authority is God given. And God gives it to those whom he knows He can. Others may try to take such authority, but they should be aware that doing so places them in a very dangerous position before God. Korah and his sons tried to assume leadership authority and were destroyed for it (Numbers 16). Saul intruded into the duties of the priest and lost his authority over the kingdom because of it (I Sam. 13). Uzziah tried to take a role of offering incense that he should not have done and was smitten with leprosy (II Chron. 26). God is very clear on the subject. He expects to be the authority giver. He will call, direct, and establish a pastor in the locale He wants him. When He does, the authority of that office will be given to the man he placed.

Now, let us deal with a concern I hear over and over. Realistically, power does come with authority, and if we follow through with placing a pastor in the position I just described, we are giving a lot of power to one man. What is to prevent him from misusing his authority? Sadly, we must admit that a person can allow himself to become negligent in carrying out his responsibilities, coming to the place where he is not fulfilling the obligations that come with the position. He could fall into immorality or other areas of sin, or he could begin to use the authority in a manner that was abusive. How does the church deal with these issues? "How does the church protect itself from this abuse?"

Honestly, I did not have an immediate answer. I spent much time asking the Lord how to have proper structure, allowing a pastoral rule, and yet balancing this with a scriptural way to deal with a pastor if there was error. There had to be a way for the church to check a pastor if any of these situations arose. At the same time the pastor's authority could not be jeopardized. My answer came in two parts. First, God dropped into my heart that the key was in this principle: Any Godly person should have no problem submitting himself to proper counsel. The second part came later as I helped the first church that came to me with a need of working on their structure, a need that required rewriting their Articles of Incorporation and By-laws. Here God helped me to see a structure that would allow the pastor, and the leadership of the church, to accomplish what we have been talking about.

I am going to include here an explanation of what this church adopted. In no way do I suggest that this is the exact structure that anyone should adopt in his or her church. It merely serves as an example to clarify my point that a pastor can have authority, and that authority can be properly checked. **This is example only!**

The church elected to have a presbytery council made up of three ministers from without the local church. These three men would be pre-named in a resolution and would be men that the pastor and the leadership (including the Board of Directors) agreed upon. The church then defined in its By-laws the details of how this council would operate. In the absence of a pastor for any reason, this council would act as executive council to the leadership, showing them how to provide ministry in the interim, as well as place the man God wanted for the pastorate. It was also detailed how the elders and the Board would work jointly to call this council together when and if the actions of the pastor deteriorated to the point that action was mandated. (The pastor could also call this council if he felt the need for advisory counsel on any matter or dispute.) This council would act as executive council, chairing every meeting, until the matter was settled. The pastor and the leadership would submit themselves to the counsel of these men, but the leadership would have the responsibility, under this godly counsel, to make all decisions and/or take any action. There were no other means available for a pastor's removal. The wording prohibited any one or two persons from acting on a vendetta and calling in these men. The leadership had to act as a team, agreeing on the action, and then contacting the council through a delegated person, with the pastor's knowledge.

Think about it. If these three men are godly men, would they listen to one or two person's complaint without going to the pastor and ethically pursuing the matter? If a dispute could be approached only under direction of this council, the leadership team is going to put much prayer and thought into actions before taking steps to call them in. Would not a pastor, who has the right spirit about him, gladly embrace the presence of godly men to aid his getting through such a situation? Would not the chairing of any meeting by men of godly caliber diffuse any vendetta and insure Christ-like conduct? The church that I was working with thought so. In fact, when I presented the details, both the pastor and the leadership were excited about setting them in, and the congregation unanimously supported their decision. (In Chapter 6 we will deal with all of the governmental structure of the local body and will cover these details in more depth.)

Having a presbytery council was not original with me. It was brought to my attention, as I was studying and praying about this area of the study, that several churches I knew of had already adopted a council such as this. In fact, I was told of one situation where having this type of council established actually diffused a church problem that could have resulted in tragedy. I solicited from these churches a copy of the section of their By-laws that

112

dealt with this. I used these examples to formulate what I presented to the church I worked with. Remember this, every church is different therefore the details of how any of this is implemented may vary. Pray and ask God what he wants for you.

It has been about four months since we finalized the structure of the church I have been referring to. I just hung up the telephone after having talked with the pastor. He wanted me to know that since the church elected to review their government and make the changes to the structure, that the atmosphere of the church had even changed. He was excited to report that there seemed to be such a solidness, a feeling that now the foundation was finally solid, and the Lord could bring revival, building on that foundation.

I rejoiced with him. Here was proof that God was blessing the aligning of the structure of the church to support the vision He wanted carried out.

God's mouthpiece.

It is God's plan to use the person He sets over people to be His mouthpiece, the person He will speak instruction and direction through. Just as the mouth is in the head of a natural body, the mouth is also going to be in the head of the spiritual body. We see an example of this in our study of Joshua. In chapter 24 Joshua speaks to the people after he has received a message from the Lord. He is not prophesying, simply rehearsing to the people the details of what God had spoken to him concerning the continuance of Israel as a nation.

I told you in Chapter 1 that I have had people come to me after I have taught this and say, "I thought God spoke to any believer." My answer was, "He does." (My thought was, "Boy, you sure didn't listen, did you!") So, I want to make crystal clear what I am saying here. God does speak to others. I am not saying that everyone except the pastor needs to be quiet in the church. I am not saying that the Lord will never give direction or speak instructions to someone else, or that that someone should not share what God did speak. Neither am I dealing here with the proper use of the gifts of the Spirit in the local body; that is another subject entirely. I am talking about how God will speak direction, vision, motivation, and detail for carrying the church forward under His care. Although God may speak this to others in the church as well, it is His plan to give the primary directions, and responsibility for those plans being executed, to the pastor.

God sets the ranks and desires organization within them. He will never reverse the principles He has instituted. I can find no example in the scriptures where God did not respect His chain of command. Because of this, the directions that the pastor receives from God will be ahead of those given to the people. This is why it is so important to pay attention to what the pastor is saying. If and when God does speak direction to someone else in the congregation, believe this. It will **never** contradict or supersede the direction He is speaking to the pastor, but rather will confirm it. Think about it. If God is speaking to the pastor, and he is hearing one thing, and God is speaking to another, and he is hearing something entirely different, then God is contradicting Himself. He cannot do that. Somebody is not hearing correctly.

In all my years of co-pastoring or associate pastoring, under three different pastors, God has never given me contradictory directions!!! He has only given me instructions that confirmed or supported what the pastor was hearing. This does not mean that every detail was the same, or that I would have taken the same exact steps in seeing it carried out. But it does mean this. The overall picture was one of co-operation and agreement. God was in it and if the details differed, we prayed until we were clear which way to move first.

I have been severely criticized many times in my past for being so "loyal." People never saw the praying and fasting and waiting on God that went on behind the scenes. They only saw that I backed my pastor in every decision, and some, who were not in concert with what God wanted to do, attributed this to "blind loyalty." I never did let this bring me to the place where I would start trying to "out hear" my pastor.

God holds the pastor responsible to lead. He is THE person to whom God is going to require an answer from concerning the people placed under his care.

Obey them that have the rule over you, and submit yourselves: for they watch for you souls, as they that must give account... -Heb. 13:17

God holds us responsible to follow that leading. Responsibility for the message shifts when the message is delivered from the speaker to the hearer. For this reason, the pastor may also need to be sensitive to the timing of the delivery of the message. Since this is so, there is a proper way for anyone else in the local body to act on what the Lord speaks to them. They should take it to the pastor and discuss its implementation before they act upon it. Just because God speaks something to us does not mean it is the proper time to implement it. It needs to be coordinated with the instructions He is speaking to the pastor as well.

For months the message I am presenting in this book burned in my heart. I knew that God had spoken for me to write it and to minister it. But before I began any of it, I sat down with Pastor Bob and talked to him about what God had placed in my heart. I would NOT go out without his support, his promotion, and the covering of my church. What I received was his blessing and his backing in all of this, as well as confirmation that it was the proper time.

I have had the sad experience on several occasions to be called into a conference, along with my pastor, by someone who proceeded to tell us what he or she was going to do. Most of the time the conversation began, "God showed me...," and they were using this statement as leverage to do something that they were going to do out from under the authority of the pastor. Their attitude was "God said...the end." In such a case the person had totally closed the door to discussion, much less counsel. Either we had to agree with them or call them a liar about hearing from God. God does not operate this way. He is not going to call a person to a ministry and have that person

115

move out from under their spiritual support to launch it. If you make the statement that God showed you, make sure that He did. The better approach is, "Pastor, let me share with you what God is dealing with me about. Would you pray about what God would have us to do, or where He would have us go from here?"

God uses many ways to speak the message He has given to our pastor. It could be a situation where the pastor stands and says, "Thus saith the Lord..." or the pastor might deliver a message on a portion of scripture that God has burdened him with. Maybe he gets the message across by teaching a series of lessons on the subject. Maybe he calls the leadership team together and implements the strategy that God has showed him, or, it could be a combination of more than one of the above. Whatever the method, the message must not be spoken with just authority, but must be spoken with anointed authority, rich in prayer, rich in wisdom, and rich in experience. We have this promise from the Lord:

> *For I will give you a mouth and wisdom, which all your adversaries shall not be able to gainsay nor resist. - Luke 21:15*

*One of the things I like to do to drive this point home when teaching a congregation or group of leaders is to ask these questions. "How many here tonight could outline the last three messages that your pastor has taught or preached? Could it be that if we cannot remember, we have passed them off as being unimportant?"

Pastor's promotion.

A pastor falls under the same principles in God's Word as everyone else, and one of these is that a person should not build himself up. So, if a pastor is to be built up, or promoted, it must come from one of three sources (actually it better come from all three):

1. His pastor. A pastor should have a pastor, and his pastor should follow the guidelines we have seen in our study of placing honor on those under him and promoting them.

2. His leadership. We have already talked much about a leader's responsibility to respect, love, and promote his pastor.

3. The congregation. The congregation should love and cherish their shepherd. We will talk more about their role in supporting the pastor and leadership in Chapter 5.

Summary.

To me, Moses always represented the true example of a pastor. He was a father figure to his people, nurturing them, and honoring leadership among them. Yet, in all his maturity, he was not so perfect that he never made mistakes.

We see a man who went to God, received instructions, and delivered those instructions to the people. I read of the accounts in Exodus where he made seven trips up and down Mt. Sinai, and I marveled at his willingness to be such an arbitrator between God and a people who were in many ways so difficult to "pastor." I stumbled at his willingness to have his name blotted from Heaven's Book if the people were destroyed, wondering how such a pastor's heart could be implanted. And then, almost by accident, I found a nugget in these passages that helped me understand. This man could have such a heart for the people because he was a man who knew God's ways, not just about his actions (Psalms 103:7). After all the trips up and down the mountain, after a conversation with God face to face, Moses still had the desire to ask God, "Show me more... (Your glory)" (Ex. 33:18).

My prayer for every pastor is that God will show you His glory, and as He does, the same love He has for the people under your care be instilled into you.

Chapter 4

OTHER LEADERSHIP MINISTRIES

We have spent considerable time talking about the many aspects of the leadership team. Then, we talked more in depth about the role of pastor in the previous chapter. But, we still have not defined the other <u>offices</u> of leadership, nor taken a look at the <u>qualifications</u> for these offices. Neither have we answered all of the questions we posed at the beginning of our study. "What does the Bible say about leadership offices?" "Is it scriptural to have the other offices we see in a church? What about elders or deacons? What about associates pastors, youth leaders, children's ministries, praise and worship leaders?"

All of these ministries make up the second element in our organization. We defined this element as **organized leadership overseen by the leader (pastor).** Remember as we study these offices of leadership that every principle about leadership that we have learned so far will apply to these leaders. They should all work together to aid the pastor in carrying out the ministry of *governments* in the local body. Also remember that they are to be appointed by the pastor with the help of the leadership team. Since we have already discussed these things, I will hold this chapter to defining the offices and listing the scriptural qualifications for these other offices. I will break the study into three topics: elders, deacons, and other supportive ministries.

Oh, one other thing. I have included quite an amount of Greek word study in this chapter. It becomes necessary for two reasons. One, the Greek word will allow us to see the most accurate interpretation of what Paul is saying. Secondly, the same Greek word is translated into different English words, so we need to go back to the original Greek to be sure of what is being said. For instance, when talking about the qualifications of an elder, the Greek word *sophron* is translated as *sober, temperate,* and *discrete.* But then, the Greek word *egkrates* is also translated *temperate.* Looking at the root words will allow us to understand the original intent of the scripture and, at the same time, avoid repetition.

Elders.

The Greek word for elders is *presbuteros,* and has been translated into several different words in the King James Bible. In some places it is used to depict seniority of age rather than respect of position. For instance, it is translated *elder* (as in *elder son*) in Luke 15:25, I Timothy 5:1-2, I Peter 5:5, *eldest* in John 8:9, and *old men* in Acts 2:7. In other places the word is used to indicate those who had risen to rank or position of leadership in the Jewish nation (some examples are Matt. 16:21, 21:23, 26:47, Mark 7:5, 8:31, 15:1, Luke 7:3, 9:22, Acts 4:5). But it is also used in the New Testament to indicate those who have been appointed this particular position of leadership to have the spiritual care of the local church (Acts 11:30, 14:23, 15:2, 15:4, 15:6, 15:22-23, 16:4, 20:17, Titus 1:5, James 5:14, I Peter 5:1).

There are two more terms in the New Testament given to this office. Both of these come from the Greek word *episkopos.* This Greek word is translated *overseers* in Acts 20:28, and is translated *bishop* or *bishops* in Philemon 1:1, I Timothy 3:2, and Titus 1:7. *Episkopos* points more to the character or nature of the work undertaken, where *presbuteros* defines the person undertaking the work.

Definition.

Elders are leaders that are appointed to the local body to oversee the carrying out of the vision and direction of the church through prayer and fasting, through teaching ministries, and through the giving of wise counsel.

Qualifications.

The qualifications for the office of elder are found in I Timothy 3 and Titus 1. It would be advisable, however, for you to study I Timothy chapters 3-6 and the entire book of Titus along with these qualifications. These chapters deal more exhaustively with areas of ministry in the church, giving a clearer picture of all the expectations for the offices.

We find that Paul lists some 24 qualifications for the office of elder in writing to Timothy and Titus. I am going to comprehensively list them here in the order that they appear. I will deal with each one in word-study form.

> *A bishop then must be blameless, the husband of one wife, vigilant, sober, of good behaviour, given to hospitality, apt to teach; Not given to wine, no striker, not greedy of filthy lucre; but patient, not a brawler, not covetous; One that ruleth well his own house, having his children in subjection with all gravity; (For if a man know not how to rule his own house, how shall he take care of the church of God?) Not a novice, lest being lifted up with pride he fall into the condemnation of the devil. Moreover he must have a good report of them which are without; lest he fall into reproach and the snare of the devil. -I Tim. 3:2-7*

> *For this cause left I thee in Crete, that thou shouldest set in order the things that are wanting, and ordain elders in every city, as I had appointed thee: If any be blameless, the husband of one wife, having faithful children not accused of riot or unruly. For a bishop must be blameless, as the steward of God; not selfwilled, not soon angry, not given to wine, no striker, not given to filthy lucre; But a lover of hospitality, a lover of good men, sober, just, holy, temperate; Holding fast the faithful word as he hath been taught, that he may be able by sound doctrine both to exhort and to convince the gainsayers. -Titus 1:5-9*

1. Blameless (I Tim. 3:2, Titus 1:6,7). Actually there are two Greek words used for blameless. In I Tim. 3:2 the word is *anepileptos* meaning *unrebukeable*. (This same word is actually translated *unrebukeable* in I Timothy 6:14.) The word used in Titus is *anegkletos* and carries the meaning *unaccused* or *irreproachable*. This is a person against whom no criticism can be made. He does not go through life with questionable conduct, always dodging definite attacks. He does not commit wrongful acts and then go to court to be acquitted. His conduct is beyond question. It would be foolish, in light of his consistent behavior, to make accusation of wrongdoing. Nothing is offered in his lifestyle for an adversary to find fault in.

2. Husband of One Wife (I Tim. 3:2, Titus 1:6). Some scholars have held that this is written to urge the elder to be married. Suggestion has been made that a married man would be more settled in his ways. The literal Greek translation is *"husband of one wife."* Paul wrote it in a time when polygamy was condoned, divorce was extremely easy, and, tragically, a wife had few, if any, rights at all. At the very least he wanted Christianity to introduce chastity. I believe the desire was for a man to be pure, moral, and devoted to his spouse in the relationship that God had planned, in a time when it was not the popular thing to do.

3. Vigilant (I Tim. 3:2). Here the Greek word *nephaleos* is translated *vigilant*. In I Tim. 3:11 and in Titus 2:2 this same word is translated *sober*. One meaning of the word is abstinence from strong drink or wine. Since Paul lists "not given to wine" separately, I believe he wanted the second meaning of the word here. That meaning is *temperate* or *watchful*. It carries with it the task of always insuring never to over indulge in anything that would lessen a person's Christian vigilance or soil his witness. Not only are we to abstain from evil but we are to abstain from every appearance of evil (I Thess. 5:22). We must weigh our actions not only against the list of sins we can identify, but against those actions' weight on our testimony and witness to the world and to younger, less mature Christians.

4. Sober (I Tim. 3:2, Titus 1:8). No, we are still not talking about drinking alcohol. This Greek word *sophron* actually means *safe in mind*. Prudent is another synonym. The same word becomes

121

temperate in Titus 2:2 and *discrete* in Titus 2:5. It speaks of a sound mind that will produce proper behavior. Literally, it is being able to have self-control, especially in the area of sensual desires. Such a contrast to today's attitude of "do anything you want." The mind will be controllable when the heart becomes fixed.

5. Of Good Behavior (I Tim. 3:2). The Greek word *kosmios* is translated *modest* in I Tim. 2:9. This is a person who is well behaved. It has been said that a person can be "of good behavior" in his outer conduct because he is "sober" in his inner life. It speaks of orderly behavior, honest behavior, showing a lifestyle that makes the person a good citizen in the land. It is displayed in the person that has a lifestyle one would desire to copy.

Many times I have made the point that every Christian should be a gentleman or a lady. It is especially important to teach this to our young people. Young men and women should show respect to those elder than them. Men, it is not going to hurt us to be courteous to ladies. Ladies...well... just act like the term implies... like ladies.

One more thought. I do not think that I have ever preached a dress code. I have certain convictions about dress, but I will not impose those on others. I do believe (and teach) that a Christian should be modest in dress as well as conduct. Our dress should reflect our Christian morals.

Well, let me get off this subject before I get into trouble...

If we look at Jesus' lifestyle, we see a person who enjoyed mixing with people. Being sober and of good behavior does not mean being a recluse or being so pious that we cannot socialize with others. Let me illustrate my point by relating one of the greatest compliments that I have ever received.

I was on a weeklong business trip in Hollywood, Florida. Each night several of us would meet to have dinner out. (I hate eating by myself.) On one of the nights at the beginning of the week, a friend of mine, who I had known for some years, invited a person he had just met that day to go with us. Several of us went to a nice restaurant where we had a wonderful time dining, visiting, and relating funny stories.

The last day of the week many of the group had returned home, including my friend. This new acquaintance caught up with me in the evening and invited me to accompany him and another friend to dinner. During the meal he made a confession. (I am paraphrasing.) "I need to tell you something. The first night we went to dinner, I accepted the invitation before I found out that you were a minister. I was so aggravated at myself, knowing the evening was ruined. I imagined having to listen to preaching most of the evening. I want you to know that I have never enjoyed visiting with anyone any more than I did with you that night. You were hilarious. You told stories and just had a wonderful time. I really did not know that a preacher could enjoy himself, nor did I know a Christian could have such fun. I thought you all just had to go around following a bunch of silly rules."

It was the greatest of compliments. My Christianity had not kept me from enjoying the company of this friend. At the same time, there was absolutely nothing in my conduct that I would have been hesitant to allow anyone to see. In addition, since he had opened the door, I had the opportunity to witness to him about how much I enjoyed my relationship with the Lord. And I did it all without being preachy!!!

6. Hospitable (I Tim. 3:2, Titus 1:8). From the Greek word *philoxenos*, this word implies *"being fond of guests."* Paul writes to the church at Rome that they should be "given to hospitality." In a time when accommodations at inns often proved to be dirty, expensive, and immoral, travelers sought other places to stay. Many times those who traveled made arrangements between families to swap accommodations. A Christian who was traveling surely needed accommodations with an atmosphere that might only be found with another believer. The word, however, goes a step farther, encompassing not being too busy to entertain someone else's needs. An elder must not only be sensitive to other's spiritual well-being, he must also be willing to take the time to minister to that person's needs, even when doing so might prove to be an inconvenience.

*My wife and I love to entertain company. Actually, we like the type of company we do not have to entertain; the kind that makes themselves at home when they are visiting. I recall having mentioned in conversation at work that we had company, and that I was looking forward to visiting with them that evening. One of the men looked at me as if I had developed a plague. He could not believe that someone would open his or her house for someone to stay. He went on to say that he cherished his privacy too much to allow someone to come into his home.

*Whether we are the entertaining type or not, whether we enjoy people in our home or not, let us never get to the place where we cannot be hospitable to others because it interferes with our privacy.

7. Apt to Teach (I Tim. 3:2). The Greek word here, *didaktikos*, means *having an aptitude to teach*. Its basic translation is to communicate or to instruct. It does encompass, but is not limited to, being able to teach by lecture. We do not have to be able to put together a formal presentation to talk about Christ. We should always seek opportunity to share Him with others, communicating Christ by living, or being, as well as speaking. We should be able to tell others around us to follow our example in the same manner Paul was able to tell the brethren at Philippi (Phil. 3:17) to follow him.

8. Not Given to Wine (I Tim. 3:3, Titus 1:7). Well, here it is. This Greek word, *paroinos*, actually translates *not given to wine*. Now, I am certainly not going to lecture or argue with you whether you should drink alcohol or not. I am going to leave that conviction between you and the Lord. (If you feel you have to justify it you probably need to refrain from it!) Let me give you a few interesting facts on the subject. In the ancient world water supplies were very inadequate, many times supplying water that was of bad taste or even dangerous. Consequently, wine became a very natural drink. It was usually drunk in the proportion of three parts water to two parts wine. Any person who over indulged in the drink was looked upon as a disgrace, even by the ordinary society, much less the Church. Terrible stories in the Bible (Noah in Genesis 9, Lot in Genesis 19, and Amnon in II Sam. 13) underscore what happens when someone chooses to indulge.

9. No Striker (I Tim. 3:3, Titus 1:7). This *"not willing"* to *come to blows* comes from the word *plektes*. As a Christian we are not to come to the place where we would go to blows or strike someone because of an argument. It has a broader application, however than just controlling our temper. It means absolutely refusing to be quarrelsome, argumentative, bullying towards others.

10. Not Greedy of Filthy Lucre (I Tim. 3:3, Titus 1:7). There are different Greek words used in Timothy and in Titus for the word *greedy* or *given to filthy lucre*. The word in Timothy is *aphilarguros* and means without *covetousness*, while the word in Titus is *aischros* or *aischrokerdes* meaning *shame* or *base*. In both interpretations the word *filthy* leaves an impression of gain by wrong means. The Lord doesn't mind us having things, so long as those things don't begin to have us, or the want of those things begin to cause us to become covetous or tempt us to acquire them wrongfully. We should never have to be ashamed of how we acquire anything, including stature or position. Care should be taken in the area of leadership to keep our motives pure, never desiring an office for self-gain. Above all, none of our gain should be acquired at another's detriment, or at the expense of our Christian ethics.

11. Patient (I Tim. 3:3). Here is another example of the English translation not being exact. The Greek word *epieikes* actually means *gentle*. (In fact, it is translated as gentle in Titus 3:2.) It means to be gentle when dealing with others, to pardon human failings by looking to the intent rather than the deed, looking at the whole rather than the part, looking at one's long-term conduct rather than one incident. Our handling of a situation should be with the motive of restoring rather than tearing down.

12. Not a Brawler (I Tim. 3:3). This word is similar to the one translated no striker. The Greek word *amachos* means to be *peaceable*. It goes beyond just controlling the situation, avoiding coming to blows. It means doing everything possible to promote peace in any situation. Keep in mind that blows can be dealt verbally as well as physically.

13. Not Covetous (I Tim. 3:3). This one is fairly straightforward. *Aphilarguros* actually means *covetous*. We are to abstain from wrong desires of wealth or possessions. We are never to be greedy.

14. One that can rule Well his Own House (I Tim. 3:4,5; Titus 1:6). The word for *rule* here, *proistemi*, is the same word used as rule in I Tim. 5:17, where it talks of elders ruling in the church. It is translated *maintain* in Titus 3:8. It is interesting to me that Paul does not just list this one, but offers more explanation, leaving nothing to be misunderstood. A person who cannot maintain an orderly household has no business trying to oversee the church. He makes it clear that our children's conduct is a good indicator of how we are doing in this area. Children that have been taught to be honest, respectful, and obedient, not children who are disobedient and unruly, will testify of a family whose relationship is typical of the one Paul is describing.

15. Not a Novice (I Tim. 3:6). The Greek word *neophutos* could have been literally translated *newly planted* i.e. *young convert*. The administration of a leadership office requires maturity. Not only would a new convert lack certain qualities that maturity brings... wisdom, experience, patience, knowledge, understanding... he would also be a more likely candidate to allow pride of that office to open an area for the enemy to come against him. We have already talked about recognizing the responsibility of being in leadership. Many times a novice has to "get the stars out of his eyes" before he can recognize the magnitude of the responsibility of the office. A person placed in a position of overseeing needs to guard against the "big head" syndrome. When we are mature enough to understand fully our inability to fulfill the calling, and God's ability to do it through us, we will be less likely to become prideful in our accomplishments.

16. A Good Report with those Outside the Church (I Tim. 3:7). There are two important Greek words here. The first is *kalos* translated *good*. Its true meaning is *valuable* or *virtuous*. The second word is *marturia* and is translated *report*. It is also translated *testimony* (Rev. 1:2, 9, 6:9), *record* (I John 5:11), and *witness* (Titus 1:13, I John 5:9, Rev. 20:4). The Greek interpretation even implies *evidence given* (as in a court of law). Combined the two words could be paraphrased, "A person who can give evidence of a virtuous record of behavior among those he interacts with outside the church."

And I think that a virtuous record anywhere is critical, but the key here seems to be "of them which are without," that is, a credible witness to those who may never see us in the church environment. Whether it is intentional or not, a person may conduct himself in the church differently than he would in everyday life. We tend to try to meet others expectations when we are around them. But, our real witness is on the job, in our community, and around our families. It is when we are having to react to everyday pressures and situations that we become unmasked. It is then that our true conduct can be observed. Here, the requirement is for the report of that conduct to be good.

I have lived all of my 40 years in the same city. From a very young age I have worked to maintain an impeccable record in my community. I enjoy being able to pick up an item at the local hardware store, even if I do not have the checkbook and need to pay for it the next day. I like being able to cash a check anywhere in town, even if the sign says "No Checks Cashed." It is great being able to buy a new vehicle without having to wait for the usual credit checks. I value the fact that my word and a handshake are a contract that many businessmen in the city will honor. I am glad I do not have to worry what a business associate may think when he hears me from the pulpit. Not only do I value that reputation, I guard it with the greatest care.

17. Holy (Titus 1:8). The Greek word here, *hosios*, is only one of several words in the Bible that are translated *holy*. It is used to describe our Lord as the Holy One (Acts 2:28, 13:35). The real implication is that we be holy by intrinsic or divine nature. Since holiness is not inherent to the carnal man, how can we be holy? Well, we are to allow the nature of Christ to reign in us by first destroying the old man (Romans 6) and then allowing ourselves to be made new in Christ (II Cor. 5:17). We should be holy in our conduct, not because it is demanded of us by Law, but because it has become our nature in Christ. The Apostle Peter brings this Old Testament (Lev. 11:44) concept to us.

But as he which hath called you is holy, so be ye holy in all manner of conversation; Because it is written, Be ye holy; for I am holy. -I Pet 1:15,16

Paul writes this to the church at Thessalonica:

Ye are witnesses, and God also, how holily and justly and unblameably we behaved ourselves among you that believe: As ye know how we exhorted and comforted and charged every one of you, as a father doth his children, That ye would walk worthy of God, who hath called you unto his kingdom and glory. -I Th 2:10-12

18. Steward of God (Titus 1:7). I know. This word is used in conjunction with being blameless. I did not list it separately in my first studies either. But when I looked more closely at the meaning of *oikonomia, stewardship,* I felt I had to list it as a qualification. A steward is a person who manages the affairs of another, either finances or property. He acts as agent for the one he is conducting business for. I think that maybe this sums up the responsibilities of an elder. He is the agent for God's business, employed to administer God's business as God would administer them Himself. Paul wrote to the church at Corinth, making a very strong statement about the stewardship of God's business. (Here the word *oikonomia* is translated *dispensation.*) He said that whether he did the work on his own free will, or if he did it reluctantly, he was still entrusted with the care and administration of the Gospel, and consequently would be held accountable.

For if I do this thing willingly, I have a reward: but if against my will, a dispensation of the gospel is committed unto me. -I Cor 9:17

19. Not Self-willed (Titus 1:7). This word, *authades*, is only used twice in the Bible. Once, here, and once in II Peter 2:10 where the writer is dealing with false prophets and teachers and where he further describes the *self-willed* as those that walk after the flesh, are presumptuous, and despise having authority over them. This word was typically used of one who was arrogantly over-bearing and set in his ways. This is the person who sets out to please himself, and have his own way, even at the expense of those around him. He is intolerant of anything he does not endorse. All of this makes him of unpleasant nature.

20. Not Soon Angry (Titus 1:7). The Greek word is *orgilos* and is only used in this verse. There is another word used in the New Testament for *anger, thumos,* which is translated wrath, indicating an anger that rises quickly and subsides as quickly. *Orgilos* differs in that it is the kind of anger that a person nurses towards revenge. It rises slowly, but becomes more lasting in nature, typifying a person who frequently holds hurts or grudges and acts vindictively.

21. Lover of Good Men (Titus 1:8). The Greek word, *philagathos*, defines a person who is a *promoter of virtue,* that is, a person who has an appetite to be around others who are of virtuous nature. It is no secret that a person usually picks up qualities, or habits, of those he spends the most time with. With that in mind, a person needs to seek out quality Christian fellowship. (The best place to do this is in the local body.)

22. Just (Titus 1:8). *Dikaios* is used frequently in the Bible and is translated *righteous* as many times as it is translated *just*. This is the person who is equitable in character as well as actions. This is the person who is observant of rule and right. It is said that a *dikaios* man renders both respect to men and reverence to God.

23. Temperate (Titus 1:8). Well, here we finally have the word *temperate, egkrates*. It implies *strong in a thing,* that is, a person who can have *self-control.* It means having self-control in our appetite for things we might otherwise indulge in. It also means having the proper self-control to not abuse the privileges of office of leadership.

24. Holding Fast to the Faithful Word (Titus 1:9). There may be those that would argue whether this is a qualification for office or merely an encouragement following the qualification list. I include it because holding fast to the faithful Word as we are taught it has two implications. First, it will enable a leader to exhort those who are around him in leadership as well as those who are under his care. Secondly, it will arm him with the necessary knowledge to be able to convince others of their need for God. Both are necessary in the office of overseeing. There are several words in this text: holding *fast* from *antechomai* meaning *adhere;* faithful from *pistos* meaning *trustworthy; Word* from *logos;* and *taught* from *didache* meaning *doctrine.* Paraphrased: We are to adhere to the trustworthy Word of God that was given to us as doctrine.

Duties of Elders.

Let me borrow from the Book of Acts one more time to begin looking into the duties and responsibilities of elders.

> *Take heed therefore unto yourselves, and to all the flock,*
> *over the which the Holy Ghost hath made you <u>overseers,</u>*
> *to feed the church of God, which he hath purchased with*
> *his own blood. Acts 20:28*

Clearly the scriptures want us to realize that these elders are to oversee the matters of the local church. (In the previous chapter I defined the role of pastor as the "chief elder.") Let me be very, very clear here: It **is not my duty to dictate nor to give strict guidelines as to HOW that is to be accomplished.** Many things may influence the organization of a church. Being under the jurisdiction of an organization may determine the exact duties and administrations of the church's governing offices. The size of membership in the church could be a determining factor in the size of the elder team, or whether a deacon team or other leadership ministries even exist. And the existence, or non-existence, of these ministries influences the duties of the elders. Certainly the pastor's leadership style will play a large role in determining how the elders are to interact with him and other ministries.

But, I am convinced that the elders, under their pastor's direction, should be responsible for overseeing all of the administrations of the local body. Every decision to build, every direction of ministry, every program... well, do you get the point... everything should be under their care. Now, if the church is able to have a strong body of deacons or other ministries, the pastor and elders may decide to delegate some of the activities out to them, or even to committees they may commission. This would allow them to concentrate on more of the spiritual needs of the church. Again, how any of this is structured is dependent on the church's individual needs. So, I am not going to tell you *how* the elders are supposed to oversee, rather that they *should* oversee.

I have had several discussions about who should be responsible for the finances of the church. Again, I cannot tell you who to charge with the responsibility of disbursing moneys. However, since finances are directly involved in the promotion of the local body's direction and vision, it is my conviction that elders should be involved. They may choose to delegate the actual hands-on to a committee, the deacons, an accountant, etc. But, they must be the ones that supervise whoever handles the matters.

The details or procedures of how this is administered have to be worked out in the church to fit its administrative needs. Remember, the church is an organization and the officer(s) acting as agent(s) on the Board of Directors are responsible for entering into most legal transactions. (I will talk more on this subject in chapter 6.)

Let me add another interesting fact. The church is recognized by the state they are licensed in as a non-profit organization. The state views it as it would any other non-profit organization. They assume the members will elect a Board of Directors, the Board will elect officers, and the administration of affairs will be vested in this Board of Directors. And rightly, the Board of Director's officers should conduct the business of the organization. But, scripturally, they should not do it without the input and guidance of the spiritual leaders of the church, the elders. How and when the elders are involved with the Board of Directors in this process needs to be spelled out very clearly. The best place to accomplish this is in the church's By-Laws or Constitution where content can be worded to assure the elders' input into this decision process of the church.

We will talk about the writing of By-Laws and Constitutions in chapter 6 of this book. But, since we are dealing with elders, let me insert here how I have seen the elders' input in the decision making process assured. We stated the usual... the administrative power of the church would be vested in the Board of Directors, the pastor being the president. The state (Louisiana) does not recognize elders so we had to go to the state's corporation laws publication to find language that the state would recognize allowing the elders' input in administrative matters. What we found is that the state does recognize advisory councils. Therefore, we appointed the elders as an advisory council to the Board of Directors. We then commissioned the pastor to bring the two bodies together as he deemed necessary to conduct the business of the church. In addition, we mandated that the elders had to act jointly with the Board in certain cases for action to be legally taken. This insured the elders' ability to have a voice in overseeing the business of the church.

One of the basic roles of elders is to support the pastor. They should be very involved with the pastor in the decision making process of the local body. Elders should, through much prayer and fasting, be able to give solid, Biblical, Spirit-led counsel to the pastor. They should be as "in tune" with the direction and the vision of the church as is the pastor. In addition, they should be able to give the fullest support to his being able to carry out that vision. Because of this, the pastor would be negligent not to interact often with this group. He should have men appointed as elders in whom he not only can place his utmost confidence, but before whom he can become very transparent. I cannot over emphasize the importance of this type of relationship. A pastor needs to be able to lean on this group for support of every spiritual nature: prayer, encouragement, fasting, wise counsel.

There are a couple of other areas that warrant discussion here. Unless the church is under the administration of an organization that will handle these situations, the elders will be responsible for filling the pastor's seat when it is vacated, and responsible for checking the pastor in the event that disciplinary action must be taken. During these times the elders will have to act without the covering of a pastor. Because of this, it is very important that all concerned know who is responsible to chair the proceedings, what the procedures are, and how these procedures should be carried out. The best way to insure that all of these things are understood and in order is for them to be written down. (Again, in the By-Laws or Constitution.) I strongly urge any church to have pre-set directions and pre-defined responsibilities written for times such as these.

If a pastor should vacate his position for any reason, the elders will need to see that the interim is filled with qualified, steadfast ministry. They will also be responsible for finding and bringing in the person God wants to fill the pastor's role. We talked about setting ministries into office in Chapter 2 so I will only remind us of the steps of the process: 1. They should go to God in prayer, asking Him to set a man over the congregation. 2. Then they must listen for His answer. This listening time is the time that they must become acquainted with the candidates. 3. When the leadership body is in agreement that they have God's direction, they should present their decision to the congregation. 4. When accepted, this person should be "set into office" before the congregation by the laying on of hands. If this process is documented, down to who does what, there will be no room for someone to cause a problem because of misunderstanding.

The filling of a pastor's position in a church is usually accompanied by strong emotions. I have seen times when these emotions can flare into problems, especially when the guidelines for action leave a lot of room for interpretation.

Although it is sad, it is a fact that there have been those who would make a play for position or power during such a time. Clearly defined criteria for who is in an authoritative position during this interim can be critical.

Elders are also given the grave responsibility of checking the pastor. Reasons for a pastor's removal should be clearly stated. When a pastor has violated the office, clear and definite steps should be defined for the elders' (and Board's) actions to remove him from office. In many organizations, the elders of a local body can go to the organization for help in this matter. If that is not available, I strongly urge the action plan to involve ministry from outside the church in the process. Having steps pre-defined and having outside ministry involved, such as a presbytery council, will assure the elders' actions are in order.

In most churches, the pastor must chair all meetings. If a pastor refused to chair a meeting to consider disciplinary action against himself, then the meeting would be illegal. Therefore, a process must exist for the elders to legally take action if necessary. At the same time, safeguards must be in place to keep one or two men from acting on a vendetta. (Sadly, these things can exist.)

I have seen a process set up like this. The elders and Board of Directors can meet one time to discuss and agree that action should be taken against the pastor. The pastor must know about the meeting. The elders and Directors can only agree to call in a pre-named presbytery board. Once the presbytery board is called, they will chair all meetings until the matter is resolved. The members of the presbytery board have no vote. They chair all meetings, provide Godly counsel, and assurance that all is done properly and in order. The pastor would then submit himself to the decision of the elders and Directors acting jointly under this presbytery council.

(I will define the presbytery board more clearly in Chapter 6. Also, I will talk more about the Constitution and By-Laws there.)

A Work Honorable and Good.

We can see in the few examples we have discussed in this section that the elders of a church have a great responsibility. I suppose that is why Paul added these words to the letter he wrote to Timothy:

Let the elders that rule well be counted worthy of double honour, especially they who labour in the word and doctrine. -I Timothy 5:17

And, that is a fitting summary to the first words that Paul wrote about the office:

If a man desire the office of a bishop, he desireth a good work. -I Timothy 3:1

The Greek translates: *a work that is virtuous and valuable.* Certainly one to be cherished and guarded at all cost.

Deacons.

The name *deacon* is derived from the Greek word "*diakonos*". It means *servant, waiter, attendant,* or *minister* and takes on the implication of dealing with the ministering to the material needs and services of the local body. These are not ordinary lay members, rather those who have distinguished themselves in their service for the Lord. We see men first set into this area of ministry in the 6th chapter of Acts, although the term deacon is not used here.

Then the twelve called the multitude of the disciples unto them, and said, It is not reason that we should leave the word of God, and serve tables. Wherefore, brethren, look ye out among you seven men of honest report, full of the Holy Ghost and wisdom, whom we may appoint over this business. But we will give ourselves continually to prayer, and to the ministry of the word. And the saying pleased the whole multitude: and they chose ... -Acts 6:2-5

I want to dispel some misconceptions about the office of deacon. Some tend to view the elder's office as a high and promoted one, and the office of deacon as a much lesser accomplishment. Well, let me direct your attention to the first thing that Paul says about them.

Likewise must the deacons be grave... -I Tim 3:8

Paul has just finished defining his list of qualifications for the elders and then he says, "In the same manner (likewise) the deacons must be honorable and honest (grave). I fully believe that it is scriptural for the deacons to be under the direction of the elders (We said that elders oversee everything.) but, I do not believe that the role of deacon is any less important. We see that Paul states that they must meet the same level of honor as well as honesty. I would argue that a deacon should meet every qualification that an elder should; not to mention that in Acts chapter 6 they appointed men that were *"of honest report, full of the Holy Ghost and wisdom"*. A deacon is just called to a ministry with a different area of focus. He is going to minister to the hands-on needs of the people. To do so, he will secure his direction and support from the pastor and the elders.

Definition.

Deacons are leaders that are appointed to the local body to support the vision and direction of the church with actions of ministering among the people.

Qualifications.

Likewise must the deacons be grave, not doubletongued, not given to much wine, not greedy of filthy lucre; Holding the mystery of the faith in a pure conscience. And let these also first be proved; then let them use the office of a deacon, being found blameless. Even so must their wives be grave, not slanderers, sober, faithful in all things. Let the deacons be the husbands of one wife, ruling their children and their own houses well. For they that have used the office of a deacon well purchase to themselves a good degree, and great boldness in the faith which is in Christ Jesus. -I Tim 3:8-13

We mentioned above that the deacon must meet many, if not all, of the qualifications of the elder. Paul, in fact, lists some of the same qualifications twice. Here are the qualifications that he lists that were already discussed in the elders list:

1. Not given to much wine (see elders' qualifications #8).

2. Not greedy of filthy lucre (see elders' qualifications #10).

3. Blameless (see elders' qualifications #1).

4. Husband of one wife (see elders' qualifications #2).

5. One that can Rule Well his own House (including children) (see elders' qualifications #14).

Paul then adds a couple of requirements that he did not include for the elders. A deacon is going to be the person who is going to have the most interaction with the congregation (maybe even the community). So, it is very interesting to note that these added qualifications are ones that would apply directly to a person who is going to represent the church to others.

1. Not Doubletongued. The Greek word here is *dilogos* and means *telling a different story.* When dealing with people, it is sometimes tempting to tell a little different story to a person to be able to agree with them or to avoid an issue. Here the Greek word means being *straight* in conversation. Not telling a person what he wants to hear, but telling him the truth in all things. Not "beating around the bush" on an issue, but clearly and fairly facing it.

2. Holding the Mystery of the Faith in Pure Conscience. Working among others is sure to provide opportunity for doctrinal discussion. It is sometimes easy to compromise in the face of peer pressure. A deacon must hold fast to those things that he has been taught, able to face all those with whom he deals with a clear conscience that he has not compromised his doctrinal position.

3. Wives. In many ways Christianity had liberated women. In a society where women lived in greatest seclusion, never asserting themselves, an emancipated woman who misused her newfound freedom might cause serious problems for the Church. Because of this, some cautions are listed here. A wife of a deacon must be mature. "Even so" (in the same way that the men are) the wives must be *grave* (*semnos* honorable), not *slanderers* (*diablolos* false accusers), *sober* (*nephaleos* temperate or watchful), *faithful* (*pistos* trustworthy) in all things.

It appears that it was very important for the wife to be in a position of good standing in the community. She would be able to aid the husband in the ministering to others' needs.

*I know that regardless of what area of ministry I have been engaged in, elder, pastor, or writer, I could not have been as successful without the encouragement and backing of my wife. And that would have been enough, but I have also enjoyed the privilege of my wife being a part of our ministry in other ways. She has provided an excellent sounding board. I have learned to respect her ability to allow the Lord to lead her, many times bringing my attention to an area I might have overlooked. She provides an excellent counseling partner, especially when there is a need for me to counsel another woman. God uses her to agree with me in prayer when ministering to others' needs.

*I won't dispute the adage "Where there is a successful ministry, there is a great wife."

I have often been asked about whether women should be appointed as elders and/or deacons. Paul makes it very clear that not only was Phebe a deaconess, but that she was to be received by the church at Rome, and that she was to receive the support she needed to carry out her business (Romans 16:1-3). Although we find nowhere in the scriptures that a woman is listed as an elder, we do find a man and wife ministry team (Aquilla and Priscilla). I have seen equally strong viewpoints for and against. I have seen women set into positions of elders and deacons and it worked well for that local church. I have seen cultures and locales where such a thing would not be permitted. So, pastor, you are going to have to allow the Lord to give you the proper convictions and the proper leading in this area.

Duties of Deacons.

The role of deacons very closely follows the definition of the office. Deacons are going to be responsible for ministering among the people to any particular need that might arise and require the attention of the church. While any spiritual counseling or ministry to "spiritual" needs will be handled by the elders, any "physical" needs will be administered by the deacons. These needs are as vital to the church continuance as any other ministry. The deacons actually become the arms of the church extended to the people both inside and outside the church body. Their fulfilling this ministry should take a tremendous load off the pastor and the elders.

You have probably caught on by now. I am not going to attempt to detail what these ministries are. They will vary from locale to locale, from pastor to pastor, from vision to vision. I do feel that the pastor and the elders working with him should define what responsibilities the deacons will have. The pastor should carry the responsibility of setting the guidelines for how the interaction between the two groups will exist. He should call the deacon team together as often as necessary to assure that they can accomplish the tasks given.

And, these details should be recorded. Again, the proper place for such details would be the By-Laws and Constitution or a procedures manual that supports the By-Laws and Constitution. Writing them down will give clarity to all involved in the process defining what is expected of the members of this team.

One more thought. Paul tells us that a person who is to be placed in a deacon position should first be *proved* (I Tim. 3:10). This supports the principle we defined of taking time to be sure the person is ready for the responsibility before placing him into leadership. This word carries the idea of a person having gone through a time of probation, or waiting, until it is evident that his life is blameless. Then, that person can be placed into position. This probation need not be a formal one with the pastor making a big point of placing a candidate on probation. I think the point is for the pastor to know the candidate, and to have observed the candidate's lifestyle long enough to be sure of the appointment before it is made. It is easier never to have appointed than to have to remove after the appointment was made in poor judgment.

139

An Acquired Standing.

For they that have used the office of a deacon well purchase to themselves a good degree, and great boldness in the faith which is in Christ Jesus. -I Tim 3:13

Paul assures us that the reward for a person who fulfills the calling to the office of deacon with all integrity will be a degree or an honorable "grade" of admiration and respectability among those who are around them. In ancient times this was considered one of the greatest of achievements and was greatly cherished.

*A company that I worked for started a program where each year an employee was chosen for recognition as an outstanding employee. The great thing was, the employee was not chosen by the company, rather by the work force. I was honored one year to be the employee that was chosen for this recognition. I still cherish it as one of the greatest things that was ever given to me, because my peers awarded it. I can tell you that Paul knew what he was talking about when he said that this type of achievement is honorable.

Other Supportive Ministries.

It does not take a lot of thought to realize that not everyone in the church that is involved in an area of ministry is an elder or a deacon. We see these other active ministries and have accepted them without question, but let us see how we can support them from the scriptures.

Just before we categorize them and go to scripture to support them, let me make a few observations. As we stated in Chapter 2, "Placing Other Leaders," these ministries should be appointed and overseen by the leadership (the pastor and the elders). They certainly should meet the criteria for membership and for leadership. Many of the same qualifications for the elders and the deacons will prove to be good guidelines for qualifying these ministries as well.

From the Five-fold Ministries.

We talked about the five-fold ministries when we were supporting the role of pastor (Chapter 3), but there could exist ministries in the local church other than the pastor that fall under this same list.

And he gave some, apostles; and some, prophets: and some, evangelists and some, pastors and teachers: - Ephesians 4:11

I am not talking about the apostles, prophets, and evangelists in particular, but as I was writing this section the Lord prompted me to add a few words about them. While these ministries are usually seen operating across the "corporate" Church, I feel strongly that they should be submitted somewhere to a local church of their own, and under the guidance and counsel of a pastor. It is their pastor to whom these ministries will be accountable to and receive support from, but I strongly feel that when they are ministering in any local church, they should submit themselves to the authority of the pastor who is there. This will not be the same degree of accountability that they will have with their pastor, but they must be willing to make themselves accountable for their actions in the pulpit of the host pastor.

But, let us talk about other ministries in the local church that may come from the five-fold ministry callings. Examples would be an associate pastor, co-pastor, or youth pastor. Although they may not be immediately filling the senior pastor role, they are still under the calling of pastor. Also, we may see those in the local church that fall under the five-fold calling of teachers. I know that there are those who interpret a calling to teach as one that is to minister to the corporate body. I will not argue the point. But, pastoring is listed in this group and it is not a corporate-wide ministry. Whether or not this teaching ministry is corporate wide, from time to time this teacher will also minister in the local body and deserves mentioning here.

From the Supportive Gifts.

There are those teachers who will teach in the local body who have a calling to the five-fold ministry of teaching, and then there are those teachers who, while they are very anointed and effective, are not called to the five-fold ministry. So, where is this supported? Well, we must point out that one of the ministries of an elder is to be "apt to teach," and we certainly will see those men called to that office who will have teaching responsibilities in the local church. But we have already covered elders, and are talking about other ministries here. We see teaching listed in what has many times been deemed the "supportive gifts."

Having then gifts differing according to the grace that is given to us, whether prophecy, <let us prophesy> according to the proportion of faith; Or ministry, <let us wait> on <our> ministering: or <u>he that teacheth, on teaching</u>; Or he that exhorteth, on exhortation: he that giveth, <let him do it> with simplicity; he that ruleth, with diligence; he that showeth mercy, with cheerfulness. -Romans 12:6-8

And teachers are not the only ministries that we see here. The word *ruleth* here literally means *to preside over* or *to be over.* I believe that it covers the areas in the church where we see a person operating in other leadership roles. Examples would be praise and worship or song leaders, choir directors, and music ministers. Any person overseeing work details or committees might also fall under this area of ministry.

I am not going to cover here the other areas listed in these verses, exhorting, and giving, because I do not classify them as leadership ministries. I will list them and this verse again when I talk about areas of working in the church, other than leadership ministries, when we talk about the congregation in the next chapter.

And, I must admit that it is somewhat difficult to know where to place some of these ministries. Maybe they fall as well under the ministry of governments:

And God hath set some in the church, first apostles, secondarily prophets, thirdly <u>teachers</u>, after that miracles, then gifts of healings, helps, <u>governments</u>, diversities of tongues. -I Cor. 12:28

While this most often refers to those who "guide" in the local church, the pastor and elders, it also refers to those who are good at organization. There are those people who have a given talent for being able to organize, steer or pilot, and oversee groups who are ministering to a particular area of need or a particular project. These ministries must not be taken lightly. A person with such an ability of administration can often accomplish with ease projects that would overwhelm others.

Conclusion.

While my list may not be exhaustive, I pray that it will give you an idea that the ministry areas in our local church are there because they are supported in the scriptures. I also pray that looking at the strict qualifications for these ministries has left you with a deeper appreciation for those who fill the ranks. And, with this deeper appreciation, you should be more mindful to support these ministries in your local church with your help and with your prayers.

Chapter 5

THE CONGREGATION

I somehow wish that I could rearrange the chapters each time that this book is opened. That way, I could be sure I was not giving the impression that these chapters were listed in order of importance. Since I cannot accomplish that, let me start this chapter by assuring you that the congregation is NOT a less important piece of our structure. As we mentioned earlier, the pastor cannot shepherd if he has no sheep.

But, the importance goes farther than just being sheep. Let us pick up our definition of this third element of our structure. The third element of our structure is **a people who can gather in unity and in support of their local body and their leadership.** In the New Testament Church we refer to this group of people as "The Congregation." We are going to see in this chapter that this group of people has great and numerous responsibilities. They are to provide an atmosphere of unity and support for each other, for the leadership ministries, and for anyone that might "come into the fold." They are to be actively involved with ministry. They will be the vehicle that will allow the leadership to move forward the vision of the local church.

Placed by God.

We talked in length about leadership ministries being sure of their placement in the area of ministry. Now I want to imperatively emphasize the importance for us, as the members of the Body of Christ, to know that we are where God wants us to be as well.

Let me start by making the point that we are not building the Church, God is.

...And the Lord added to the church daily such as should be saved. - Acts 2:47

And believers were the more added to the Lord, multitudes both of men and women. -Acts 5:14

And I (Jesus) say also unto thee, That thou art Peter, and upon this rock I will build my church; and the gates of hell shall not prevail against it. -Mat 16:18

Knowing that Jesus is putting together His Church like He wants it does not mean that we can kick back and allow Him to do all the work. Contrarily, it means that every believer has the responsibility to prayerfully seek out God's direction for the local church where He wants them to become a member. The one thing of surety in a Christian's life should be, "God put me here and I'm going to be here!" In fact, if God never called us to a leadership ministry in the local church, it is still vital that we know we are where God wants us to be. Why? Because it is not always going to be easy sailing. There will be times of troubled seas, for whatever the cause. If we are never sure of anything else, we need to be certain that for the long haul, for the short haul, in good times, in bad times, in prosperous times, in lean times, in times of abundant rain, in times of drought, we are going to stand in the knowledge that we are where He has us, and we are going to support those in authority over us as we stand.

*I have seen my share of "pop-corn" Christians. Those are the ones who "pop up" here and want to be totally involved... until the first time something does not suit them. The next thing you know they "pop up" in some other congregation.

*While these are not hard and fast rules, there are several observations I have made about such people. Usually, they come on very strong. "God has sent me here with _____ ministry." Listen, even when God did move me from one church to another with the calling to be involved in ministry, I did NOT go tell that pastor that I had come there to do that. I went there, letting the pastor know that I was being led of God to come and submit myself to his leadership and to be committed to the

145

church. The pastor knew God wanted me in the leadership role and placed me there.

*Also, I have noticed that most of these "pop-corn" Christians have trouble submitting to any kind of authority. They generally have the attitude that they are too advanced spiritually to have to have leadership over them. Let me be plain. I have little use for people in the ministry that have the attitude that they are superior in their calling and need no pastoral covering.

*I have also noted that the first time that something doesn't go just their way, these people seem to "get a word from God" to move. These same people generally make the rounds, moving from one church to another as soon as something does not suit them. Many times the pattern repeats itself in each church they move to.

*I know that many of the things I have said here seem harsh. Believe me, I long to see these people in a place where God can use them. But, they cannot be used so long as they continue to operate with these attitudes, and lack of willingness to submit to leadership authority.

And, not only does each member need to know what local body the Lord wants him to be a part of, he needs to know what part. Let me explain. The local church is made up of many members, but they all fit together to make up the body.

For as the body is one, and hath many members, and all the members of that one body, being many, are one body: so also <is> Christ. -- For by one Spirit are we all baptized into one body, whether <we be> Jews or Gentiles, whether <we be> bond or free; and have been all made to drink into one Spirit. -I Cor 12:12, 13

But speaking the truth in love, may grow up into him in all things, which is the head, <even> Christ: -- From whom the whole body fitly joined together and compacted by that which every joint supplieth, according to the effectual working in the measure of every part, maketh increase of the body unto the edifying of itself in love. -Eph 4:15,16

Peter uses another analogy comparing the church to a house that must be built up:

Ye also, [as lively stones], are built up a spiritual house, an holy priesthood, to offer up spiritual sacrifices, acceptable to God by Jesus Christ. -I Peter 2:5

Whatever the comparison, the important thing is that we know which part of the local body we are to fit into, and that we know each part carries the same importance. There is not one of us that would be willing to part with a piece of our natural body, no matter how small and insignificant it might seem. Let us ask the Lord to help us adopt the same attitude about the body of Christ and the parts that make it up (especially our local body – our church home).

Characteristics of a Strong Congregation.

I imagine that we all have the same desire: that our church be able to grow. To do so, it needs to be strong and healthy. What are some of the characteristics of a strong congregation? Let us look to God's Word.

1. A United People.

I once heard this question asked, "Are you a group of individuals, or are you an individual group?" I recently traveled by airline and had to spend a layover sitting in the terminal. As I sat there I was part of a group of individuals. Each of us was doing our own thing, going our own way. Although we had something in common (all of us waiting for a plane), we were not working together in any fashion. We had separate routes, separate destinations.

We need to be an individual group. This does not imply that our group will not interact with others (we better!); I am not discussing church fellowship here. It means that every one of us in the local body has common goals and is working jointly to see those goals met. It also means that we enjoy fellowship with each other. I am convinced that to be able to work in unity is God instilled. Yet, I also believe that the best way for us to continue to be united is to practice. Practice gathering together and allowing God to flow in our midst until we are like the first church of the New Testament. Until we are all in one accord and in one agreement. Such unity carries with it great effects:

Cause:

And these all continued with one accord in prayer and supplication... -Acts 1:14

And when the day of Pentecost was fully come, they were all with one [accord] in one place. -Acts 2:1

Effect:

And suddenly there came a sound from heaven as of a rushing mighty wind, and it filled all the house where they were sitting. And there appeared unto them cloven tongues like as of fire, and it sat upon each of them. And they were all filled with the Holy Ghost, and began to speak with other tongues, as the Spirit gave them utterance. -Acts 2:2-4

Cause:

And they continued stedfastly in the apostles' doctrine and fellowship, and in breaking of bread, and in prayers. -Acts 2:42

And they, continuing daily with one [accord] in the temple, and breaking bread from house to house, did eat their meat with gladness and singleness of heart, Praising God, and having favour with all the people. - Acts 2:46-47

Effect:

And the Lord added to the church daily such as should be saved. -Acts 2:47

Cause:

And by the hands of the apostles were many signs and wonders wrought among the people; (and they were all with one accord in Solomon's porch. -Acts 5:12

Effect:

And believers were the more added to the Lord, multitudes both of men and women.) -Acts 5:14

Cause:

But we will give ourselves continually to prayer, and to the ministry of the Lord. -Acts 6:4

Effect:

And the word of God increased; and the number of the disciples multiplied in Jerusalem greatly; and a great company of the priests were obedient to the faith. - Acts 6:7

Cause:

And the people with one accord gave heed unto those things which Philip spake, hearing and seeing the miracles which he did. -Acts 8:6

Effect:

For unclean spirits, crying with loud voice, came out of many that were possessed with them: and many taken with palsies, and that were lame, were healed. And there was great joy in that city. -Acts 8:7-8

Remember that this principle applies to the congregation as well as the leadership ministries: there is no such thing as a "one-man show."

2. A People with an Ear.

I was once told of a study that was conducted. In the study a device was used to measure energy exerted by different persons. These devices were placed both on the speaker and the listener. Shockingly, it was recorded that the listener exerted the most energy. It takes effort, because a good listener is not just one who lets what he hears "go in one ear and out the other." Rather, a good listener seeks to retain what he has heard to put it to work for him at some point in time.

God set scripture in the New Testament for us to see that the Church gave an ear to what was being said to them.

And they continued stedfastly in the apostles' doctrine and fellowship, and in breaking of bread, and in prayers. -Acts 2:42

And the people with one accord gave heed unto those things which Philip spake, hearing and seeing the miracles which he did. -Acts 8:6

We also see this displayed in the Old Testament, first by the people who had gathered to listen to what Joshua was going to say.

And Joshua said <u>unto all the people</u>... -Joshua 24:2

And then we see it in even greater display in the people of Nehemiah's time. We see that they met, not because it was expected of them, but because they desired to hear from God.

And all the people gathered themselves together as one man into the street that <was> before the water gate; and they spake unto Ezra the scribe to bring the book of the law of Moses, which the LORD had commanded to Israel. And Ezra the priest brought the law before the congregation both of men and women, and all that could hear with understanding, upon the first day of the seventh month. And he read therein before the street that was before the water gate from the morning until midday, before the men and the women, and those that could understand; and the ears of all the people were attentive unto the book of the law. -Neh.. 8:1-4

We see one more thing about Nehemiah's congregation. They allowed the Word they heard to affect them.

For all the people wept, when they heard the words of the law. -Neh. 8:9

And, they left there with an understanding of the word that had been presented.

And all the people went their way to eat, and to drink, and to send portions, and to make great mirth, because they had understood the words that were declared unto them. -Neh. 8:12

They were good listeners.

I am compelled to be repetitious here, saying something that I have already said when talking to the leadership, because I want the rest of us to know it is applicable to us as well. God uses many ways to speak the message He has for us. It could be a message where the pastor stands and says, "Thus saith the Lord..." It could be that the pastor delivers a message on a portion of scripture that God has burdened him with. Maybe he gets the message across by teaching a series of lessons on the subject. Maybe he calls the leadership team together and implements the strategy that God has showed him. Maybe it is a combination of more than one of the above. Whatever the method, we must realize that God is speaking and strive to hear what God is saying to us individually as well as corporately.

3. A Supportive People.

By definition the congregation will not only be a people who are united, they will be a people who are supportive. Supportive of what? The leadership. The vision and direction of the church. Each other. They have to be a people who will give their voice and their actions to show their commitment to serve.

Notice that Joshua did not just deliver the message to the people and assume they understood and agreed. He brought the message to a point several different times where the people would have to respond. Listen to the dialect (paraphrased). "Choose today who you are going to serve" (24:15). "God forbid that we should leave serving Him to serve other gods" (24:16). "If you forsake the Lord, He will consume you" (24:20). "No! We will serve the Lord" (24:21)! "Do you give yourselves as witness of this decision" (24:22)? "Yes! We stand as witnesses" (24:22).

Voicing our agreement is vital. What we say about our leadership or our church can build or destroy. Showing our support by our actions is just as important. There is truth in the old adage, "actions speak louder than words." Are you willing for your voice and your actions to stand as testimony of your support?

And Joshua wrote these words in the book of the law of God, and took a great stone, and set it up there under an oak, that <was> by the sanctuary of the LORD. -- And Joshua said unto all the people, Behold, this stone shall be a witness unto us; for it hath heard all the words of the LORD which he spake unto us: it shall be therefore a witness unto you, lest ye deny your God. -Joshua 24:26, 27

*I have found time and again that it is much easier to stand if everyone fully understands your position. Having voiced that position often times helps us not to be "wishy-washy." It alleviates the temptation to change in face of pressure. Often I have thought that it would be a great idea for us to "bill-board" our decisions to serve the Lord.

Did Israel's decisions that were voiced to Joshua and the leadership have an effect on the nation? I think so:

And Israel served the LORD all the days of Joshua, and all the days of the elders that overlived Joshua, and which had known all the works of the LORD, that he had done for Israel. -Joshua 24:31

4. A People of Prayer.

Maybe it should say A *People of Prayer and Study.* I stress continually to our congregation that they cannot maintain a healthy body by eating spiritually three meals a week. (Just try eating only three natural meals a week and see how you fare.) We must maintain a regiment of personal prayer and study of God's Word.

You know, I find nowhere in the scripture that God apologizes that we have to spend time in prayer. Communication is necessary for any relationship. I have explained this point to my son and daughter like this. "How would you feel if your very best friend would not speak to you? How long would you remain friends? What if I never spoke to you? Could we enjoy each other's company? Would I be able to know what's going on in your life? How could we continue to be close in relationship?" The same principle applies to our relationship with God. He wants to be the "Friend that sticks closer than a brother" (Prov 18:24), but the rest of that scripture says that if we are to have friends we must be friendly. I submit that we cannot be friendly if we have no communication, and that such communication is vital to our friendship with the Lord.

Paul sums up the four areas of a Christian's prayer life in his letter to Timothy:

I exhort therefore, that, first of all, supplications, prayers, intercessions, and giving of thanks, be made for all men: -I Tim. 2:1

I do not want to get into a lengthy teaching here on prayer, but I feel it necessary to point out the differences in these words.

1. Supplications are requests made in earnest. They represent one of the basic forms of prayer life in our Christian walk, requiring little maturity to make. In fact, our first request for salvation was a supplication. Supplications are neither bad nor to be left behind as we grow. We will continue to make supplications a part of our prayer life throughout our relationship with the Lord. Unfortunately, some people just never advance from this level of prayer life, to include the other three areas.

2. Prayers are the acts of approaching God with the intent to develop a relationship. This is where we hold communication with God, intimately spending as much time as needed to develop a close, personal relationship. It is the personal part of our prayer life. A person can make supplication for you but they cannot develop a relationship between you and God.

3. Intercessions are also requests, but on a different order. This time the petition is going to be submitted by entering into the King's presence and personally making the presentation. It implies having the "clout" or relationship that affords us the ability to have entry into the court of the king. Our clout is not in ourselves, but in the righteousness of the Son of God who is seated at the right hand of the Father and not only has invited us into His presence, but will present us as well.

4. Thanksgiving is not only a type of grateful language to God, it is also an act of worship. Basic thanksgiving comes with contentment. Are we content in our relationship with the Lord? Mature thanksgiving comes at all times in all situations (Eph. 5:20). If our next blessing was contingent on the thanks and praise we gave for the last answer to prayer, what could we expect?

Let me conclude this list by saying this. I find no other support that I would embrace and cherish more than I would a congregation's prayer support. I personally know of times in my ministry that the difference in whether I made it through a situation or not was dependent on the faithfulness of the people who held me up in prayer.

Called to Minister.

Albeit we are not called to a leadership role in ministry, every person in the congregation **IS** called to minister.

Ministry of Reconciliation.

Paul in writing to the church at Corinth makes clear the fact that we are all called to the ministry of reconciliation.

And all things <are> of God, who hath [reconciled] us to himself by Jesus Christ, and hath given to us the [ministry] of [reconciliation] -II Cor 5:18

Let us define reconciliation to fully understand what the apostle is saying to us. It is the realization on the part of a person that they are sinful and alienated from God, and the act on their part of accepting the provision that Jesus has made for them to be forgiven of their sins and to be justified in God's sight. Paul further writes to the church in Corinth that we are to be ambassadors for the Lord (II Cor. 5:18-20), bringing to the world the news of this reconciliation. Do we represent the Lord as an ambassador would represent his country? You should be out there in the community representing Him. You should be bragging on <u><your church name></u> Church. You should always be sharing what God is doing in your church, in your life, and what He can do in others' lives if they will let Him.

Ministry of Helps.

The ministry of helps has been defined as ministering in the local church by way of rendering aid or assistance. Helping what? Helping the five-fold ministries. Helping the leadership. Helping others.

> *And God hath set some in the church, first apostles, secondarily prophets, thirdly teachers, after that miracles, then gifts of healings, **helps**, governments, diversities of tongues. -I Cor 12:28*

It includes within its ranks ushers, secretaries, cleaning personnel, sound equipment operators, caretakers of the lawn. It encompasses all ministries that, although they are not leadership roles, are vital to the job being accomplished. It is here that much of the load is taken off the shoulders of the leadership.

Ministry of Supportive Gifts.

I must repeat a portion of scripture that I used in the previous chapter. These are the verses from Romans that list areas of ministry sometimes referred to as the supportive gifts. In the last chapter I talked about *teaching* and *ruling*, both which place a person in leadership areas of ministry. (Also note that the *ministering* in this scripture points back to the office of deacons.) I now want to look at three other gifts that are very important areas of ministry in the local church, but may not place the person in an area of leadership. They are: *exhorting, giving,* and *showing mercy.*

> *Having then gifts differing according to the grace that is given to us, whether prophecy, <let us prophesy> according to the proportion of faith; Or ministry, <let us wait> on <our> ministering: or he that teacheth, on teaching; Or he that <u>exhorteth</u>, on exhortation: he that*

giveth, <*let him do it*> *with simplicity; he that ruleth, with diligence; he that* showeth mercy, *with cheerfulness. -Romans 12:6-8*

The original Greek for *exhorteth* could actually be translated *to call to one's side* or *to one's aid*. It is descriptive of that person who has the ability to minister consolation or who is able to give comfort. This person will be quick to see the hurt of another, genuine in his interest of that hurt, and able to articulate comfort to the person in need. Going beyond that, this person will be the type to give encouragement to those who are struggling as well as praise to those who are doing a good job. The impact of such a ministry in a congregation can hardly be measured.

The gift of *giving* certainly includes but is not limited to monetary giving. It actually translates *to share earthly possessions,* and speaks of meeting needs, with money and/or services. This is not just a giving of our extra or our leftovers, but a sharing of those things that we have been blessed with when it is needed to meet the needs of another. And, we can not weigh monetary giving over services rendered. This giving is to be done with little fanfare. That is, the ability to give should bring glory and honor to the Lord who has blessed with the ability to do so, not gain attention for the giver.

*I know of a businessman in my hometown who runs his own air conditioning and electrical business. His practice, when doing work for a church, has always been to not charge for his labor, and in many instances furnish some of the materials. While this is more of a services rendered type of giving, I can assure you that more than one church body has been appreciative of the blessing.

The last, but certainly not the least, of these three ministry gifts is the gift of the *showing of mercy*. Here we see a ministry of actually *performing acts of kindness*. This ministry may very well overlap either of the two we have already mentioned. In other words, an act of kindness may be to encourage or to exhort. It could be to give to a need. However, it does cover any act that will render a blessing to someone else: a meal cooked for someone who has extra company, a house cleaned for someone who has been ill, a night of babysitting to allow a couple some free-time, a yard mowed, a cake baked, a card sent...

In the church that I attended a few years ago there was a widow who would send a card to different ones as she felt a need to do so. I remember that I was going through a very trying time and was somewhat discouraged (yes, pastors get that way from time to time too). It just happened that on one particular morning I retrieved an envelope from the mailbox, and upon opening it found a card. It was a very simple card with a very short message, "I was just thinking of you and of how much I appreciate you and all that you do. In His love," I can't remember the design of the card, and the wording here may not be exact, but I will never, never forget how much that card meant to me. As I stood there in the yard with tears rolling down my face I knew someone had cared; had cared enough to send one small card.

It will be almost impossible for the pastor or his leadership team to see every need in the local body. Nor can they tend to every need that they see. The larger the body grows the more evident this becomes. I believe this is the very reason the Lord gives these gifts to the church. They are precious gifts that will not only minister to the needs or the congregation, but will take a tremendous load off the leadership team. Pray that the Lord will raise up such men and women in your congregation, and rejoice and praise Him when you see it done.

Pastor's Responsibility.

I have talked about the pastor's responsibility to the leadership ministries. Now let me say a few things about his responsibility to this congregation. All of the points I list here can be rolled up into the ministry of shepherding the people, as their pastor must have a love for the people much like the love that is demonstrated by Moses.

And it came to pass on the morrow, that Moses said unto the people, Ye have sinned a great sin: and now I will go up unto the LORD; peradventure I shall make an atone-

157

ment for your sin. -- And Moses returned unto the LORD, and said, Oh, this people have sinned a great sin, and have made them gods of gold. -- Yet now, if thou wilt forgive their sin--; and if not, blot me, I pray thee, out of thy book which thou hast written. -Ex. 32:30-32

I know that the longer a pastor is at a church, the more the love for the people will grow. But I also know that there is a burden, a love, a feeling for the people of a congregation that is deposited into the heart of a pastor by the Lord when he becomes their pastor. In fact, I think this is one way a pastor knows that he should be there. This deposited love goes beyond any developed love.

What are some of these shepherding responsibilities? Let us see.

1. He is to teach them and nurture them. A pastor must be sensitive to the leading of the Lord to be able to know what diet the people need. He may find those who need the milk and those who need the meat. He must encourage as well as teach. A person can not exhort someone to do something that he has not been taught to do. However, after that person is given the skills to accomplish the task, proper exhortation is essential.

2. He is to correct them. Here is an area that no shepherd wants to have to minister. But many times correction is vital to growth. It could be vital to the safety of the individual, or it could be vital to the church's development. Error left unchecked will hinder at the least, destroy if it grows. When a pastor sees a person in a dangerous situation, he has the obligation to counsel that person into an area of safety. Sometimes, correction is a part of that counsel. Whatever the degree of correction, it will be accomplished with much more acceptance if the pastor displays an attitude of love.

I have been placed in the situation as a pastor to have to correct. I have found that there is no substitute for praying before any action is taken, and acting under the direction and guidance of the Holy Spirit when action is taken.

There have been times when the Lord would reveal the consequences of the person not taking corrective counsel. I can tell you that there is nothing that will tear the heart out of a pastor

any more than having to allow a person to go through those con-
sequences because they would not listen to corrective counsel.

3. He is to involve them. This handshakes with teaching and nurturing. But, a pastor must learn to present the need and the vision for meeting the need to the people in such a way that they will want to become a part of what is being done. Nehemiah sets an example.

> *Then I told them of the hand of my God which was good upon me; as also the king's words that he had spoken unto me. And they said, Let us rise up and build. So they strengthened their hands for this good work. -Neh 2:18*

Whether the people see these goals and desire to be a part of them may depend upon the pastor successfully presenting them before the congregation.

> *And the LORD answered me, and said, Write the vision, and make it plain upon tables, that he may run that readeth it. -Hab. 2:2*

The pastor should utilize his leadership team to accomplish all the things that we have set forth here as his responsibilities.

The Result.

What can we expect to see as result of a group of people standing together, working together, supporting one another in the work? Well let us go back to our congregation in Joshua's time, the nation of Israel. We see two results of their efforts:

1. They all shared equally in the victories and spoils as they entered Canaan land.

2. They all received their inheritance.

The closer we get to the Lord's return, the more we will see a deterioration in the climate of the world, and the more we will need each other.

> ***Not forsaking the assembling of ourselves together, as the manner of some is; but exhorting one another: and so much the more, as ye see the day approaching. - Heb 10:25***

Chapter 6

GOVERNMENTAL STRUCTURE

Explanation.

Maybe the last thing an author should do is admit that he had to make some adjustments in an area that he was writing. But, since I don't know any better than to admit it... I sought God's help in making sure that the things I say are both scripturally sound and balanced. And, God did give me balance in how to approach this chapter. Let me explain:

I think it is safe to assume that all of us want our churches to operate based on the scriptural requirements we have learned so far. At the same time, however, there are certain requirements that a church must meet in order to be recognized by the state and the federal government. To better accomplish this, the church can become incorporated. Upon being incorporated certain offices and some structure is imposed. For lack of a better term, I will refer to this part of the church's structure as the *"governmental structure."* Although governmental structure is not the main focus of this book, I felt compelled to discuss it because it directly affects how the church operates. So, I set out to "storm the gates!" I intended to research the ONE and ONLY right, ideal way to have a church structured and demand no deviation!

In fact, in the original draft of the outline for this book, this was Chapter One. Thank God for a pastor who brought up the question of what area of the book God wanted the greatest emphasis placed. As I progressed, I realized that emphasis had to be on the leadership principles from His Word. An understanding of these principles, mixed with prayer and waiting on God for direction, should enable us to wisely adopt the structure that He would be pleased with for our particular needs.

But, we cannot ignore those "legal" requirements either. So, I felt the Lord prompting me to develop an understanding of the composition of the incorporation, and how to blend it with God's requirements. I have been writing on this book for almost two years, and my research into this area has been ongoing the entire time. After multiple calls to the state and federal offices, reading and re-reading of legal material, multiple discussions with an attorney, bouncing back and forth between conversations with pastors, and actually having "hands-on" experience in putting together this structure for a church, I finally felt I had some understanding of the requirements.

*As I have stated in other areas of this book, my ministry has been one of helping other churches. A part of that ministry has been to fill in as interim pastor in different churches, with the responsibility of bringing in a pastor. These times almost always demanded that I go to the church's Articles and/or By-Laws to develop an understanding of how to operate within them. In addition, there have been those times that I was involved in adopting changes to both of these documents to bring them closer in line with the needs of the church and/or scripture.

*Even as I was writing this I had the privilege of helping a church work out its structure. I was asked by the pastor (and the Board of Directors) to review their Articles and By-Laws. Many changes had been made to these documents over the years and they felt a need to comprehensively review what they had. This review revealed a need for the church to completely rewrite both documents, aligning them legally and scripturally. After several months of working with the pastor, the Board of Directors, and a Christian attorney, the church unanimously, and excitedly, adopted the new documents.

*The timing was God-sent! Everything I write here is refreshed and highlighted by the experience of having recently completed the entire process. As I go through the pieces, I will share with you many of the things that I learned.

But the more I learned, the harder I found it to set ultimatums of what this structure needed to be. One of the first things that the

Lord made clear to me was that He simply wanted me to translate what I had learned in my research into language that might be a little easier to understand. Admittedly, this governmental area is a very confusing one, filled with legal jargon and many times misunderstood by even pastors and leaders. I have seen Godly men, men who knew what the vision for their ministry was and how to carry it out, not have a clear understanding of how these requirements impacted their structure. My goal here is to define the different pieces that make up this structure so that all of us can have a better understanding, not **to dictate their use**.

He also let me see that there was a variety of interpretation about how this "legal" structure was to harmonize with Scriptural requirements. I found churches with structure that I did not deem as the *ideal* Scriptural structure, and was confused to see that it worked very well for them. Now understand. I am not talking about areas of operation that violate Scripture. I am talking about areas that simply leave room for different interpretations. (Remember, not all this "legal" stuff is spelled out in scripture.) Let me give you a couple of examples why a church may display a particular type of structure.

First, what works in one local body may not work at all in the next. God knows this and often times leads accordingly. Remember what I said earlier, the Rules are the same, the implementation of those Rules may vary. For example: I have seen churches where women were set into leadership areas and not only was it accepted by the congregation, but it was a great strength to that local body. I have also seen geographic areas where the mind set, or culture, of the people was such that a pastor would be impeached (if not worse) for even mentioning such a thing. Remember what we said about God placing pastors. I have seen pastors whose personality made them ideal for a congregation in one locale, but who would never be able to pastor a people in another. All of these things play into the final structure of the local body.

Secondly, church structure may be inherited. Unless a pastor is starting a work from scratch, he most certainly will inherit some incumbent structure, and this structure may fall somewhat short of what he might interpret as being best. But, incumbent structure many times reaches into the hearts of those who have been at the church for a length of time and it might take years for that structure to be re-molded. In fact, short of a miracle, that structure may never be changed. Another example: While I personally find no support in the Scripture for congregational nominations to fill church offices, I see churches that operate that way. Generally, even if an amendment to change this practice could be approached, it would take the congregation's vote to accept the amendment. In effect, this congregation is being asked to vote to never be able to vote again. Realistically, this may never happen. So, does God throw them to the wind because of the way they operate? No, He may just place a pastor there with wisdom and ability to work within this structure.

Please Listen!

Again, **I wish I could raise my voice!** I am <u>NOT</u> here to dictate a structure or to set rigid rules. My responsibility is to define the different pieces and requirements, helping you to acquire a better understanding of them. If you are in an area of leadership that will make some of the decisions, the responsibility of how these pieces fit into your structure and the effect they have on the implementation of your day to day operations falls on your shoulders. If your are not in a leadership area, a clearer understanding of these things will enable you to be more supportive to the leadership in their implementation.

Requirements will vary from state to state. All of the research that I did on this subject was with the State of Louisiana and my examples will reflect such. However, the requirements will not be drastically different, and the terminology will be similar enough for this information to be of benefit no matter what state you may be working in. Again and again I will strongly urge you to use this study <u>**only**</u> as a guideline, and to acquire the services of a good attorney when going through the process. This attorney will be able to give you the specifics of any differences for your state (or situation) and will be able to make sure all the legalities are in order.

To Write or Not to Write.

That is the question. Should a church have written By-Laws in addition to its Articles of Incorporation? How much detail should go into these documents? These are questions that usually surface in the beginning of any discussion about this topic. I originally took the stance that I see many pastors take: write as little as possible so that no one can hold you to it. I have moved away from that position for several reasons.

When a ministry becomes incorporated, it will become a non-profit organization, and as such, will have to operate under the guidelines imposed by the state. Many of these guidelines can be changed in the Articles of Incorporation or By-Laws, however, any area that is not spelled out in these documents must use these default guidelines. As we continue through this chapter we will discuss some of these defaults and give suggestions of areas that might need to be detailed differently.

I have also been involved in administering the rules set forth in By-Laws only to find that they were very vague and left room for too much interpretation. And, in any time of discord, you can count on someone else interpreting differently for you. There has to be a balance of defining thoroughly enough to make sure the intent is clear to all, and yet not dictating such rigid rules that there is no flexibility left for the Lord to lead. Prayerfully seek His will for this balance. I find that He is as willing to give leadership here when details of operation are defined as He is to give it on a daily, operational basis. Remember, we did say that He is an organized God and if He sets the structure it will also remain spiritual.

Let me further this point by saying that the time to set these guidelines down is a time when all is going well: before the pastor leaves, before a problem arises, before a rule needs to be enforced...you begin to get the picture... while all the leadership team is working in harmony, set these guidelines. They should be developed and adopted while all are in agreement, and then used to bring us through the test when all are not.

And, everything needs to be plainly understood. I believe this to be a scriptural guideline. There is a principle that we see in both the Old and New Testament of everything being done in the presence of two or three witnesses (Deut. 17:6, 19:15; Matt. 18:16; II Cor. 13:1; I Tim. 5:19; Heb. 10:28). Oh, be practical. We know we do not go out and bulletin board every detail concerning operations in the church. But this scripture suggests that we do not run around implementing the operations of the church secretly either. It would do us well to follow the instructions given to Habakkuk.

And the LORD answered me, and said, Write the vision, and make it plain upon tables, that he may run that readeth it. -Hab. 2:2

Defining the Structure.

As I define church structure, I realize that there are those churches that, although they are affiliated with an organization, operate independently, basically governing themselves. I also know that others are under organizations that play a more aggressive role in how the church operates. In fact, the organization may dictate much of the local church's structure. At some level, however, these different pieces will need to be implemented, and an understanding of them will help us either implement them or operate under them.

Check the Internet.

One more thing. If you have Internet capability, check to see if your state has a web page for the Secretary of State office. Louisiana, for example, has such a web page and it offers numerous services. Information about the corporation such as the registered agent, the Incorporators, the officers, and the operation status can be checked. In addition, many of the necessary documents for filing information (including Articles of Incorporation) can be downloaded at no charge, along with the instructions for using them. Other instructions and procedures can be obtained as well.

The Incorporation.

There are two forms of organizations available, the unincorporated association and the corporation. Usually, both are recognized by the state. When a group of people begin to meet and operate as a church, they are an unincorporated association until they obtain recognition from the state as a non-profit organization, a corporation. As an unincorporated association, the church can obtain an employee identification number from the state, and automatically have federal tax exemption without having to apply with the IRS.

It would be advisable, however, for a church to incorporate for several reasons. First, the corporation enjoys provisions for its members against liabilities. A Corporation acts as a *"person"* or entity. The corporation, not individuals, makes all legal transactions; therefore any litigation against these transactions would be against the corporation. The Incorporators, directors, and officers of the corporation can claim the benefits of the limitation of liability contained in the provisions of the state's statutes. In addition, it is often much easier for a corporation to meet the requirements for ownership of properties, etc. than it would be for an individual or a trustee of an unincorporated association. Ownership is kept in the organization's name, not a person (could circumvent serious ownership disputes). Also, a corporation provides for a defined person of contact, making communication much easier for the state, federal government, and/or businesses.

Articles of Incorporation.

To become recognized as a corporation, the church must file a copy of its Articles of Incorporation with the state. The instructions for filing should be requested from the Secretary of State office. (In Louisiana this must be filed with the State of Louisiana, Secretary of State, Corporations Division. It must be filed with an affidavit of registered agent and the appropriate filing fee.) When accepted, the church will be recognized as a non-profit organization, and all the rules, as well as privileges, will be applicable. Be sure to check whether one of the multiple originals or a certified copy needs to be recorded with the county or parish after it is received from the state.

The state may provide a form that can be filled out in lieu of filing written Articles of Incorporation (titled *Articles of Incorporation* [R.S. 12-203] in Louisiana). This form meets only the minimal provisions required by law to be set forth in the Articles of Incorporation. It is strongly advised that you secure an attorney's help in writing and submitting Articles of Incorporation for your church, rather than submitting this form. This will assure that all legal aspects are covered, and will afford the opportunity of deviating from state defaults as needed. Since the language of the Articles of Incorporation is legal in nature, an attorney's help there is invaluable.

Many times the thought of having to go to an attorney to set in "spiritual" matters for your church seems unappealing. Let me say this. Any legal transactions of the organization are going to require proper legal counsel. I strongly urge you to develop a rapport with a respectable attorney at an early stage. I know from experience that there are good, Christian attorneys available that will be of invaluable benefit.

Each organization's needs should be looked at specifically when creating the Articles of Incorporation. These articles are going to "lock in" the basic structure of the organization. Specific areas where the organization wants to operate differently than the state's defaults need to be detailed. Because of this, careful thought needs to be given to the wording, clarity, and depth of the provisions. Many of these details can be included in the Articles of Incorporation or they can be spelled out in the Constitution or By-Laws. A good "rule of thumb" is to ask this question. "How hard do you want it to be to make a change to a particular area?" Since changes to the Articles will require an amendment to be filed with the state, and By-Laws require only a resolution to be adopted in the local church, it is obvious that things that need to be "set in concrete" need to be in the Articles. It is not uncommon for the Articles of Incorporation to outline the "skeleton" of the structure and the By-Laws to fill in the meat. In the By-Laws more detail can be given to the definition of offices, procedures, and operations of the organization.

Most often the state can furnish a list of basic requirements that need to be included in the Articles of Incorporation. I have included here a checklist of points that might be included in your discussion with your legal counsel when developing your Articles of Incorporation. This list is NEITHER all-inclusive nor exhaustive. Use these only as a guideline, being careful to check your state's requirements for any differences. (I have included a sample copy of Articles of Incorporation in Appendix A.)

- The name of the corporation.
- The initial registered office and address of the corporation.
- The full name and address of each registered agent.
- The full name and address of each incorporator.
- The full name and address of each initial director and the term of office. (Include the office title of those who have been named officers.)
- The federal tax identification number of the organization.
- A statement that the organization is a non-profit corporation.
- A listing of the purposes, powers, and objectives of the corporation. (A mission statement, statement of whether the organization is on a stock basis or non-stock basis, a statement to have and exercise all rights and powers conferred upon a non-profit corporation, and a statement of adherence to the IRS 501(c) (3) taxation rules.)
- A statement that the duration of the corporation is perpetual.
- Statement of membership. (Usually state here that the default rules of the state are going to be overridden and the standard of membership are going to be set out in the By-Laws.)
- Define the board of directors. (Define here the number of directors, how they are to be appointed and approved, who is to act as chairman of the board, how directors are to be removed. Also define how officers are to be elected. State

that the administrative affairs of the corporation shall be vested in the Board, and define a quorum. It might be advisable to state here that the length of office will be set in the By-Laws.)

- Define how amendments are to be made to the Articles of Incorporation. (The state's corporation laws will determine how amendments are made unless otherwise stated here.)
- Define how amendments are to be made to the By-Laws. (This detail could be included in the By-Laws, but as we stated earlier, becomes more concretely set here.)
- A statement that claims the benefits of the limitation of liability contained in the provisions of the state.

Sometimes, the Articles of Incorporation for a ministry, especially a local church, can become quite hard to follow if a considerable number of amendments have been made over the years. In such a case, the organization can submit a new set of Articles as a Restated Articles of Incorporation. Correct wording needs to be placed in this document to assure the state that this new document encompasses the entire text of the original articles as amended by all amendments, except the names and addresses of incorporators and directors. The entire document can be reworded but must sum the original and all changes. Be sure to check with your legal counsel to make sure of all legalities for your state <u>before</u> attempting to do this (see Appendix B).

By-Laws.

The By-Laws or Constitution is a document that can be adopted by the organization to further detail its offices, operations, and procedures. This is the place where more definition can be given to offices and how they are to be structured. The organization may decide to include much of its operating procedures here as well. (Sometimes these operating procedures are separated in a *Operations and Procedures* manual, leaving only the definition of the offices and structure here in the By-Laws.) These By-Laws need to be as detailed as necessary to clarify the rules and regulations of the organization, being specific enough to that organization's needs to make provisions for its carrying out the vision and purpose that God has ordained for it.

As I did with the Articles of Incorporation, I am including a checklist that outlines some of the specifics that might be considered when preparing the By-Laws. I strongly suggest these By-Laws be reviewed (if not written) by legal counsel for their legal content before they are adopted. Also, I have included a sample By-Laws in Appendix C. Again, do not use this sample as one to fit your procedures to, but rather as a check list of items that might be included when writing By-Laws to fit your procedures.

I found that the attorney was very willing to write the Articles of Incorporation since there are very specific guidelines from the state as to the content, and the variations from those guidelines by the organization easily understood. He was, however, more reluctant to write the By-Laws, considering the specific needs of each organization will greatly differ. (Not to mention the wide interpretation of scriptural principles, etc.) I did find him more than willing to review the By-Laws that I had put together for legal content. If you face writing your By-Laws because of this same situation, I urge you to use an existing document for an outline and make the necessary changes for your structure rather than starting from scratch. Then review them with legal counsel for accuracy.

- Define the location of the principal office of the corporation.
- Define the corporation's right of government. (Right to govern by New Testament scripture, right to purchase, sell, acquire, etc.)
- Tenets of Faith.
- Define membership. (Remember that we overrode the defaults of the state by declaring that we would define membership here. List qualifications for membership, define how they are to be recognized, and define how membership can be lost. If the structure of the church is a congregational form of government set the voting age and define the vote.)
- Define all offices. This includes the Board of Directors term of office (we defined the Board in the Articles of

Incorporation.), the pastor, elders, deacons, presbytery board, etc. (Define the office, how it is to be filled, the duties and responsibilities of the office, and how its members can be dismissed.)

It is not a requirement that this document be filed with the state or the federal government. It is imperative that a copy of the By-Laws along with all amendments be kept in such a manner that all know it is current and comprehensive. It would be a wise move to register a copy with your legal counsel to assure that all know it is the current copy. The By-Laws can be completely replaced if they become so encumbered with amendments that clarity is an issue.

Policy and Procedures Manual

Sometimes it is desirable to have a third document for your organization, the *Policy and Procedures Manual*. We have already stated that the Articles of Incorporation are the "bare bones" or skeleton of the organization. This document needs to be conclusive enough to define the organization to the state, but not so inclusive that every time there is a policy change the state has to be sent an amendment. It should "lock in" the basic structure, overriding any defaults that need to be overridden on the state level to allow the organization to exist as needed. The By-Laws then add some "meat" to this skeleton. That is, they further define the offices, how they are established, and their primary duties.

But many times, especially in larger churches, there is a need to spell out in great detail the policies for certain operations of the church. This detail can be documented in a policies or procedures manual. This detail could be included in multiple sections of one document, or it could be written in multiple documents, each detailing a specific subject or area of operation. For example, the church may have the need to detail criteria, steps, training, classes, etc. for becoming a member. They may need to have guidelines for the nursery area, guidelines that include the responsibilities both for the parent and for the attendant. Operating procedures may need to be laid down for handling of the finances within the church. I could list more, but I think this will give an idea of what could be included.

This area is like any other area we will talk about in this section. The structure will be determined by the need. And, as you grow, the changing needs may require these documents be revisited. Policies and procedures change, and for that reason, there needs to be a clear predetermined method (policy) defining who can make these changes and how.

Board of Directors and Officers.

Let me first list some of the things that the state may assume if they are not spelled out differently in the Articles of Incorporation or the By-Laws.

The state may not care what the title of these directors are, but usually default the administration of the affairs of the corporation to them. The state may set the minimum number of directors on the board, the default term of office, and the maximum length of term. They also default how the directors are to be elected. Let me give you some examples, again using Louisiana as the reference. The state of Louisiana assumes that the administration of all affairs will be invested in the board of directors. The directors shall hold office for one year and cannot be elected for a longer single term than five years. The voting members of the organization shall elect these directors. All of these directives, except the maximum single term, can be changed in the Articles of Incorporation or the By-Laws.

The state may also require the board of directors to elect officers. The minimum number, the titles, and whether a person may hold more than one office are usually set by the state. The state also lists some of the responsibilities and authorities of these officers.

*Here is where a bit of confusion sometimes exists. I have had churches (pastors) tell me that they do not have a board of directors, just officers of the corporation. My answer is, "Yes you do." If the number of board members and the number of officers are the same, with each holding a title of office, then it

172

may appear that all you have are officers, but the state recognizes these men as a board of directors as well.

Most often, these officers consist of a president, a secretary, a treasurer, and one or more vice presidents. Unless otherwise stated, the president, or by resolution of the board, the president or vice-president of the corporation shall have the power in the name and behalf of the organization to conduct legal transactions. Any changes to the board of director members or to the officers positions needs to be reported on the next annual report to the state. (In Louisiana this report is Form 389 Rev. 3/94.)

Having said all I have said about the board and the officers as pertains to the state let me now add a little commentary about their affect on the church. Basically, this board and its officers are going to represent the local church to the business world. They will make the decisions and carry out the legal ramifications of those decisions. For that reason, I argue that the members of this board should be godly men. In fact, I believe they should be elder and/or deacon material. I also believe that the pastor should be the president of the corporation, the person with authority in all areas, and the chairman of all meetings.

According to most state defaults, these directors are nominated and elected by the members, or the congregation. I do not believe this is the best method for securing nominations, since congregational nomination generally leads to a popularity contest. In such a nomination there is the assumption that every member has prayed, is being God-led, has an understanding of leadership requirements, and knows the lives and hearts of those they are nominating. Most of the time, this just is not the case. So, I suggest much prayer and thought be given to changing the default of how these men are nominated. Allow the pastor, or the pastor and the elders, or the pastor and the board and the elders, to seek out these men and present them to the congregation. If the structure of the church determines that the congregation needs to be involved (congregational government) let them ratify the leadership's nominations. This procedure should assure that the men placed in the directors' seats are men the leadership knows meet the scriptural requirements for such leadership positions.

Agents.

Here is another area that might cause confusion. *Agents* and *registered agents*.

The registered agent(s) of a corporation is that person(s) reported to the state who will be recognized as the contact person for the corporation. (A registered office address must also be supplied.) The appointment of a person as registered agent does not in itself empower that person to be able to make legal transactions for the corporation. Their main purpose is to provide the state a person and place of contact for all communication. Their authority to perform duties for the corporation can be decided by the directors. Any change to the registered agent and/or office must be reported to the state, usually on the annual report.

One or more agents (different from registered agents) can be defined by the By-Laws or by the board. These agents are the persons that (are defined by the By-Laws or by the board to) have such authority and perform such duties in the management of the property and affairs of the corporation as deemed necessary. By default, the president, or president and any vice president shall have this power. The directors can, however, by resolution empower someone else to act as agent.

Since the president often acts as agent and as registered agent, these two offices sometimes are confused.

Advisory Council.

Provision can be made in the Articles or the By-Laws for the church to have available advisory council(s). This would make counsel available for the "legal" structure, the board of directors and the officers, and/or for the "scriptural" structure, the pastor and the leadership. Since most of the time these positions overlap, counsel should be provided for both.

From the very beginning of my study and my working in the area of church government, the Lord kept stirring a question in my heart. Scripturally the pastor is to set in elders who would help direct the direction and decisions of the local church. The state, however, does not recognize the elder team. Instead, they look to the directors, who according to them, are elected by the members. So, the state saw a membership-electing-directors-setting-in-officers structure. The Bible sees a leader-set-over-leadership-directing-the-congregation structure. How could these two co-exist? How could the "legal" structure be made aware of the elders' input into leadership?

Remember, the pastor has the responsibility to set in elders as God leads. The limitations of how many can be set in and their term of office is not imposed on elder leadership, as it is with directors.

My study led me to see that the state does recognize the corporation's right to govern itself, including the definition of committees or advisory councils. So, in the By-Laws we were able to define the elders' offices scripturally, and then name them as an advisory council to the directors. We stated that the pastor had the authority to bring in the elders at his discretion to work with the directors on any matter. We further detailed that certain actions of the directors **required** a joint decision of the directors and the elders. (Such as bringing in or removing a pastor.) This assured "legal" representation of the elders in the administration of the church's affairs as is scripturally mandated.

The same could be done for the deacons. Their involvement in any part of the church's organization can be spelled out as well. In fact, other committees or advisory councils could be formed as needed.

In discussion of the pastor in Chapter 3, we defined another council, the presbytery council. This is a council made up of ministers outside the local church to aid the leadership from time to time as is needed. Although we defined this council in that chapter, I feel that I should include the information here to be comprehensive when covering advisory councils.

175

This presbytery council should consist of several ministers (usually 3 to 5 in number) from without the local church. The pastor and the leadership (including the directors) should determine the persons filling the offices. This should be accomplished in a meeting, and the names of these men recorded in the minutes of that meeting. (The men would have to be contacted and agree to be a part of the council before this resolution could be made. This would require more than one meeting to accomplish.) The office and the duties of this presbytery should be defined in the By-Laws. Such definition needs to include when and how this council could be brought together, as well as their responsibilities and authority when they are brought in.

This group of ministers would provide an invaluable asset to the pastor and leadership. They could call upon this council's support and direction at any time they deemed necessary. In addition, it could be mandated that this council plays a role in the church's business under certain conditions. For instance, if the church had a conflict that seemed unresolvable by the pastor and leadership, this council could be brought in for godly direction (or arbitration). If the pastor's actions deteriorated to the point that the leadership felt action had to be taken, strict guidelines could be set detailing how and what could be done to secure this council's help in the matter.

In the Appendix A and B of this book I have included a set of Articles of Incorporation and By-Laws. In the By-Laws you can see the wording detailing how this council can be utilized. Notice that it takes a joint effort of the elders and the board of directors to appoint someone to contact the council. This assures that one or two people are not acting on a vendetta to hurt the pastor.

Think about it. If I am on such a council (and I am), and I was contacted by the representative of the church, I am not going to take any action except to make sure the council comes together and conducts themselves according to the guidelines for their involvement and according to scriptural ethics. My first question is going to be, "Is all of the leadership in agreement that this council needs to come together?" My second response is going to be to remind them that nothing else should take place until they do. This insures that, from the beginning to the end, the matter is handled in a godly fashion.

Let me not leave this subject on a negative note. The pastor and leadership body should be ecstatic about having such council available to them. This council does not have to be there just for the problem times. They could be used any time the church feels they need input from their presbytery. This could be the giving of prayer and counsel support throughout a decision making process or any project. It should also provide security for the church to know that although the pastor is given his proper authority in the local body, he has also placed himself in a position of accountability if the need arises.

*Having a presbytery council was not original with me. It was brought to my attention, as I was studying about areas of church government. From the beginning the idea was one that I embraced. Several churches that I know have such council set in, and I have heard stories how this council diffused problems that could have otherwise been tragic for the church.

*In some of the churches, this council not only has the authority to come in and chair the meetings when a situation arises, they also have the authority to make the final decisions concerning the situation. In the church that I worked with to set this into for the first time, the Lord led us to not give the final decision making to this council. Here was the reasoning. This council is going to come in, help get through the situation, and then leave the church to be guided by its leadership. The leadership should make the decisions that they are going to have to operate under. The council was charged with chairing any meeting, giving godly counsel, and leading any discussions that needed to be led. The leadership team was charged with making the decision. If they cannot make sound, godly decisions under the guiding hand of this presbytery council, then something is amiss.

*Every church is different and because of this the details of how this is implemented may vary. Prayerfully seek God for what He wants you to install.

And, counsel being defined in the By-Laws is not limited to the type that we have described here. God may lead you as pastor to have available other types of counsel. The important point is this... Have godly counsel available. It is scriptural. In I Kings 12 we see that a king, Rehoboam, literally lost the kingdom because he chose to ignore wise, seasoned counsel. When determining who should be the person(s) named as those you will go to for counsel, be sure they are men of season, men of caliber, men of faith. Even men like Paul and Barnabas returned to the elders and apostles at Jerusalem and submitted themselves to the decisions made (Acts 15).

Do not let these men appointed as a presbytery council be strangers to your church. Bring them in from time to time and allow them to minister to the congregation. Set time aside for your leadership team to interact with them. Allow the church to see that these are men that they can place their confidence in at any time.

Tax Exemption and IRS Status.

Another area that needs understanding is the corporation's status with the state and federal governments. There are several pieces to this status.

First, before the corporation (or unincorporated association) can pay wages, an employee identification number (EIN) needs to be obtained from the IRS. (In Louisiana this is the 72-xxxxxxx number.) This number must be supplied on the Articles of Incorporation. It can be obtained by filing a Form SS-4 application with the IRS. The form contains the necessary instructions for completing this process.

According to *Publication 557, Tax-Exempt Status for Your Organization*, from the federal government, churches automatically have a 501 (c) (3) tax exemption status with the IRS without having to actually file for the exemption letter. The IRS maintains two basic guidelines:

That the particular religious beliefs of the organization are truly and sincerely held, and

That the practices and rituals associated with the organization's religious belief or creed are not illegal or contrary to clearly defined public policy.

There may be certain advantages in going through the steps to receive the exemption letter. Certain organizations may require the letter before they would recognize the exemption. To obtain the letter the corporation must first obtain their employee information number. Then they must complete *Package 1023, Application for Recognition of Exemption* and file it along with *Form 8718, User Fee for Exempt Organization Determination Letter Request,* and the appropriate fees. This application must also be accompanied by a conformed copy (a copy that agrees with the original and all amendments) of the organization's Articles of Incorporation and the Certificate of Incorporation. By-Laws are not mandatory, but a conformed copy that an authorized officer certifies as current can be included.

State income tax exemptions need to be checked with your particular state. (The State of Louisiana will follow the exemption status that the federal government has determined.) Also, state sales tax exemption should be checked. (Currently there is not exemption status for a church non-profit organization in the State of Louisiana.)

*Be sure to check the state's tax exemptions. If they are unclear, allow your legal counsel to aid you. Also check for other exemptions. For instance, recent legislation in the State of Louisiana (1996) has been passed to allow churches to buy literature, including songbooks and Bibles, tax-free. This is not a tax number, but rather a certificate of exemption. To obtain this certificate, the church must file form **Application for Certificate of Authorization** with the state. This application is available from the State's Department of Revenue and Taxation.*

Summary.

I pray my motive has been very clear. It is impossible to define the different pieces without giving examples for clarity. But, my examples are just that -- examples. The state and federal government will dictate some of the legal structure to you. Some of that structure can be changed by addressing specifics rather than operating under the defaults. Other changes are needed to align this structure scripturally. The definition of the structure should embrace the carrying out of the vision of the ministry.

I want each of you to have a better understanding of all the requirements and how they affect your organization. Even though these requirements may vary from state to state, the definitions here will aid you in understanding what they are. Remember this. Do not do it alone. I did not. I sought both godly counsel and legal counsel to help me understand what needed to set into order. If I aid another church in this area, I will solicit legal aid again. I encourage you to do the same.

Chapter 7

THE FINISHED WORK

In the last chapter of the book of Exodus it is recorded that "Moses finished the work." Not his life, nor his ministry, just the task that God had assigned him to do at the time. God had given explicit instructions on how the tabernacle was to be built and over a period of several months, under Moses' supervision, that work was carried out. In many ways this chapter is similar. The Lord dealt with me about penning this material, and now I am concluding that work. And, unless you are one of those people who read the back of the book first, you have just finished reading the things that He has made very dear to my heart. Whenever I am scheduled to speak somewhere, I pray, "Lord, don't let me just 'preach' Your Word, but let me, under the anointing of the Lord, see Your Word ministered to the hearts of Your people." It is my sincere prayer that as you have gone through this material, the Lord has done the same.

It is great when we can stand and admire the finished work. Although we won't ever finish the entire Work, there will be many times when we can see a particular goal reached, a mile-marker go by, having been able to finish what God had instructed us to do. And, it is at such times that we stop and reflect. I do not imagine there are any of us who, when looking back, can find nothing we would not change. There will be those things that we would do differently given the chance. But, most of the time things cannot be done over, so instead of looking back, we must press on, using what we have learned to lessen the mistakes as we go. I am convinced the principles in this book can help you do just that.

When Moses finished the tabernacle, the glory of God so saturated it that he could not even enter into it. Moses had seen the majesty of God on the mountain, had even talked to God face to face, yet when the finished product was there, the anointing and the glory of God was so much more dynamic! All he had to do was finish.

But, how can we be assured that we will be able to finish the work God has given us to do? Well, Paul said, "*I press toward the mark for the prize of the high calling of God in Christ Jesus*" (Phil. 3:14). He knew that the only way for him to see the finish line was for him to continually press into God's enabling. Sometime ago the Lord dropped into my heart a line that I have printed in the leaf of my Bible and refer to from time to time: "I AM NOT VITAL TO GOD'S MINISTRY; HE IS VITAL TO MINE." It reminds me that if ever I am going to be successful in finishing what God has asked me to do, I am going to have to depend on His enabling power. My responsibility can be summed by the writer of the book of Ecclesiastes: "*Fear God, keep His commandments: for this is the whole duty of man*" (Eccl. 12:13).

I can hardly wait to get somewhere, to start something, to meet someone, but, I always have trouble saying good-bye. I struggle now, with a lump in my throat, to find an adequate way to close this book. Let me do so by praying, for every person who reads this book, the prayer that Paul prayed for his readers:

That the God of our Lord Jesus Christ, the Father of glory, may give unto you the spirit of wisdom and revelation in the knowledge of him: The eyes of your understanding being enlightened; that ye may know what is the hope of his calling, and what the riches of the glory of his inheritance in the saints, And what is the exceeding greatness of his power to us-ward who believe, according to the working of his mighty power, -Eph. 1:17-19

And, like Paul, I will covet but one thing from you...YOUR PRAYERS!

Appendix A
ARTICLES OF INCORPORATION

Included here is a copy of a set of Articles of Incorporation that I have recently submitted for a church. Information in the brackets < > would need to be information specific to the organization that they are being submitted for.

Please keep three things in mind as you review these. First, they are here for example only, and are not supplied as a fill-in-the-blanks-and-submit form. Secondly, they were designed to support the structure needed to carry out the vision of the church they were written for. And lastly, they were written in the state of Louisiana and are designed to meet the requirements imposed by that state.

Use these as a guideline. Prayerfully ask the Lord to give you wisdom to make the changes necessary to meet your needs. Pen these needs to the best of your ability, and then secure the help of legal counsel to complete them. Let your counsel know you are depending on them for all legalities, especially state specific ones.

Articles of Incorporation
of
<Corporation name here>

Article I.

The name of the corporation: <Name of corporation>

Article II.

Mailing address of Corporation: <Address>
                                        <City, State Zip>

Article III.

Office Address: <Address>
                              <City, State Zip>

Article IV.

Federal Tax ID: xx-xxxxxxx

Article V.

Initial Board of   <Name>   **President**
Directors: <Address>
                        <City, State Zip>

                        <Name>   **Vice-President**
                        <Address>
                        <City, State Zip>

                        <Name>   **Vice-President**
                        <Address>
                        <City, State Zip>

                        <Name>   **Secretary**
                        <Address>
                        <City, State Zip>

                        <Name>   **Treasurer**
                        <Address>
                        <City, State Zip>

Article VI.

Incorporators: <Name>
                        <Address>
                        <City, State Zip>

                        <Name>
                        <Address>
                        <City, State Zip>

Article VII.

Registered agent(s):   <Name>
                            <Address>
                            <City, State Zip>

Article VIII.

The Corporation is a non-profit corporation.

Article IX.

The period of its duration is perpetual.

Article X.

Purposes and Powers:

A. To conduct, carry out, and further a Christian Ministry as God so directs, and specifically to advance the gospel of Jesus Christ.

B. To establish a non-denominational church, open to all worshipers of the Christian faith. To provide, in an atmosphere where Jesus is Lord, an established place of regular congregation praise and worship services, Christian instructional facilities for all aspects of the members, including the young in age and young in spirit, and the establishment and dissemination of a doctrinal code or creed based upon the inerrancy of the Word of God.

C. The corporation is not organized for pecuniary profit nor shall it have any power to issue certificates of stock or declare dividends, and no part of the net earnings of the corporation shall inure to the benefit of, or be distributable to, its members, trustees, officers or other private persons, except that the corporations shall be authorized and empowered to pay reasonable compensation for services rendered and to make payments and distributions in furtherance of the purposes set for in **X. A** and **X. B** hereof. Said corporation can make distributions to organizations that qualify as exempt organizations under section 501 (c) (3) of the Internal Revenue Code.

D. To have and exercise all rights and powers conferred upon non-profit corporations under the laws of Louisiana, or which may hereafter be conferred, including the power to contract, rent, buy or sell personal or real property, to publish a newspaper or magazine, to own and/or operate radio or television stations, support missionaries, raise funds, and to do those things necessary to promulgate the Gospel in an effective and efficient manner. Notwithstanding any other provision of these

185

articles, this corporation shall not, except to an insubstantial degree, engage in any activities or exercise any powers that are not in furtherance of the purposes of this corporation.

E. The Corporation shall not conduct or carry on any activities not permitted to be conducted or carried on by an organization exempt from taxation under Section 501(c) (3) of the Internal Revenue Code and its regulations as they now exist, or as they may hereafter be amended, or by a corporation, contributions to which are deductible under section 170(c) (2) of the Internal Revenue Code and Regulations as they exist or as they may hereafter be amended.

F. The Corporation has the right to govern itself, including the right to make rules, regulations, and establishment of offices as are defined in its Constitution and By-Laws.

G. Upon the dissolution of the Corporation, the Board of Directors shall, after paying or making provision for the payment of all of the liabilities of the corporation, dispose of all the assets of the corporation exclusively for the purposes of the corporation in such manner, or to such organization or organizations organized and operated exclusively for charitable, educational, or religious purposes as shall at the time qualify as an exempt organization or organizations under section 501 (c) (3) of the Internal Revenue Code, as the Board of Directors shall determine.

Article XI.

A. Membership. The standard of membership shall be set out in the Constitution and By-Laws of this Corporation.

Article XII.

Board of Directors:

A. The administrative affairs of the Corporation shall be vested in its Board of Directors pursuant to Acts 6:3, composed of the pastor of the congregation, who shall act as chairman, and four (4) members of the congregation, to be appointed by the pastor, approved by a majority of the Directors, and subject to ratification by majority vote of the congregation.

B. Each director shall hold office for a period of time as shall be specified in the Constitution and By-Laws, or until he resigns. Any director who fails to uphold the standard of membership as defined in the Constitution and By-Laws shall be removed from office by the remaining Directors.

C. A majority of the Directors shall constitute a quorum, for the transaction of any and all business, by the Board of Directors.

D. The pastor of the congregation shall fill the office of President and shall act as chairman for the Board of Directors. Other officers can be elected by a majority of the Board of Directors.

Article XIII.

A. Amendments to the Articles of Incorporation. Any amendments to the Corporation's Articles of Incorporation shall be adopted by a majority of Directors present at any regular meeting or at any special meeting, if at least five days' notice for any intention to alter, or amend the Articles at such a meeting is given to each of the Directors. Any amendment adopted by a majority of the Directors must be ratified by a majority of the members. A vote shall be taken at a meeting after the intent of the meeting has been announced in three (3) consecutive services.

Article XIV.

A. Amendments to the Constitution and By-Laws. Any amendments to the Corporation's Constitution and By-Laws shall be adopted by a majority of Directors present at any regular meeting or at any special meeting, if at least five days' notice for any intention to alter, or amend, or repeal the Constitution and By-Laws, or adopt new bylaws as such a meeting is given to each of the Directors. Amendments adopted by a majority of the Directors must be ratified by a majority of the members. A vote shall be taken at a meeting after the intent of the meeting has been announced in three (3) consecutive services.

Article XV.

A. Liability of Incorporators, Directors, and Officers. The Incorporators, Directors, and Officers of this corporation claim the benefits of the limitation of liability contained in the provisions of Louisiana R.S. 12:24 (c) to the fullest extent allowed by law as fully and completely as those said provisions were cited herein in full.

STATE OF < State >

COUNTY (or PARISH) OF < County or Parish >

THUS DONE AND PASSED on this _____ day of _____, 20XX, and in the presence of the competent witnesses, who hereunto sign their names with the said appearers, and me, Notary Public, after due reading of the whole.

Witnesses: < Corporation Name >

_____   _____

                                    By: < President >

_____

BEFORE ME: _____
                          Notary Public

Appendix B
RESTATED ARTICLES OF INCORPORATION

To submit to the state a completely new set of Articles of Incorporation, the organization must send them in as Restated Articles. This very well could be an exact copy of the original set along with a copy of each and every amendment as it was made. The state should already have these documents, but they could be sent again as Restated Articles to assure that all the above has been combined into one set.

I have, however, seen a situation where the organization desired to completely replace the original Articles and amendments with a rewritten document that included all the above, (and any new amendments made at the time) in a document that was easier to read. To do so there were some things that had to be done differently than if original Articles were being submitted.

The title should be **Restated Articles** and there is some state required information that needs to be written at the beginning of the document. Also, **Article V. Initial Board of Directors** in the Articles of Appendix A should be replaced with **Article V. Current Officers** (a list or names and addresses should be provided). Also, **Article VI. Incorporators** should be replaced with **Article VI. Board of Directors** (a list or names and addresses should be provided).

The following example shows the information that had to included at the beginning of the document. **This is intended as example only. Details may vary from state to state and situation to situation. Be advised that proper legal counsel should be used when any change is made to your Articles.**

Restated Articles of Incorporation
of
<Corporation name here>

BE IT KNOWN, that on the date hereinafter provided, BEFORE ME, the undersigned Notary Public, duly commissioned and qualified in and for the County/Parish and State hereinafter provided, and in the presence of the competent witnesses hereinafter named and undersigned, personally came and appeared, <President's Name>, President of the Corporation, a person of full legal age and resident of <County/Parish>, <State>, who declared that the following Restated Articles of Incorporation are those pursuant to LSA-R.S. 12:241, AND THAT THE FOLLOWING Restated Articles of Incorporation are those authorized by that certain Resolution passed unanimously by the Membership of the Corporation on <date>. The original Articles of Incorporation were dated <date>.

The Restated Articles of Incorporation accurately copy the original articles and all amendments thereto effective at the date of the Restated Articles of Incorporation, without substantive change except as made by any new amendment or amendments contained in this restatement. Each amendment herein has been effected in conformity with law.

Appendix C
CONSTITUTION AND BY-LAWS

The copy of the By-Laws included, like the Articles of Incorporation in Appendix A, was recently submitted for a church. Once again, use these only as a guideline to aid in compiling a set that would support your ministry. The same admonitions I gave at the beginning of Appendix A for the Articles of Incorporation apply here as well.

Constitution and By-Laws
of
<Corporation name here>

Article I.
OFFICES
Principal Office

1.01   The principle office of the corporation in the Sate of Louisiana shall be located at <street address> in the city of <city>. The corporation may have such other offices within the state as the board of Directors may determine or as the affairs of the corporations may require from time to time.

Article II.
RIGHT OF GOVERNMENT

2.01   <Corporation name> shall have the right to govern itself according to the standards of the New Testament scriptures, "Endeavoring to keep the unity of the Spirit in the bond of peace...till we all come in the unity of the faith and the knowledge of the Son of God, unto a perfect man, unto the measure of the stature of the fullness of Christ." Ephesians 4:3-13

2.02 This church shall implement its New Testament Christianity commissioned by the further prerogatives:

1. To establish and define policy by which it shall be governed.

2. To designate its own officers. To establish and maintain such departments, institutions, committees, and services within the fellowship for the propagation of the Gospel and its work embraced by the purposes of this corporation. To arrange for its own meetings, and to govern itself in accordance with the constitution and bylaws herein and after defined;

3. To administer the regular ordinances defined in this constitution;

4. To establish other churches, Christian schools, missions, and Christian centers both at home and abroad according to standards set forth in the New Testament and/or any and all such other vehicles as may be deemed appropriate and advisable by the Board of Directors and the Elders;

2.03 In connection therewith, or incidental thereto, it shall have the right to purchase or acquire by gifts, bequest, or otherwise, either directly or as trustee, and to own, hold in trust, use, sell, convey, mortgage, lease, or otherwise dispose of any real estate or chattels as may be necessary for the furtherance of its purpose; all in accordance with its constitution and bylaws or as the same may be here afterward modified or amended.

Article III.
TENETS OF FAITH

3.01 The following Tenets of Faith provide a foundation of Biblical truth upon which the members of this body of believers can build their Christian life.

1. THE SCRIPTURES. We believe the Bible to be the inspired Word of God. (II Tim. 3:16, II Pet. 1:21)

2. THE GODHEAD. We believe there is One God eternally, existent in three persons: The Father, The Son and The Holy Spirit. (Deut. 6:4, Matt. 28:19, Luke 3:22, Eph. 4:6)

3. THE FALL OF MAN. We believe that in the beginning God created man innocent, pure, and holy, but through the sin of disobedience, Adam fell: hence by one man's disobedience, sin entered into the world. (Gen. 1:27, Rom. 3:23, 5:12)

4. REDEMPTION. We believe in repentance to God, confessing ourselves as sinners, receiving forgiveness through the Lord Jesus Christ. We believe that our redemption is through the blood of Jesus Christ and Regeneration of the Holy Spirit. (John 3:3-5, Acts 2:38-39, 11:18, 17:30, Rom. 5:1, II Cor. 5:15-21, Gal. 2:16, 3:13, I Peter 1:18-19, Tit. 2:14, Rev. 5:9)

5. WATER BAPTISM. We believe in water baptism, by immersion, in the Name of Jesus according to His command into the Name of the Father and the Son and the Holy Spirit, and that this baptism is commanded by Jesus and identifies the Believer with His death, burial, and resurrection. (Matt. 28:19, Mark 16:16, Acts 2:38, 10:48, 19:5)

6. THE HOLY SPIRIT. We believe the Baptism in the Holy Spirit with the evidence of speaking in other tongues is for all believers. (Acts 2:4, 39)

7. SANCTIFIED LIFE. We believe that true believers will live a sanctified life hating sin and loving to please the Lord. (II Cor. 7:1, I John 3:2-3)

8. DIVINE HEALING. We believe that God is still the healer of His people, and that Jesus' redemption provides healing for the mind and body. (Ex. 15:26, Isa. 53:4-5, Mark 16:18, James 5:14-15, I Peter 2:24)

9. COMMUNION. We believe that all followers of Christ should partake of communion, or the Lord's supper, in remembrance of His death until He

comes again. (Matt. 26:26-28, Luke 22:19,20, I Cor. 11:23-34)

10. TITHES. We believe that tithing has been ordained of God to act as provision for His work. (Gen. 14:20, Num. 18:26, Deut. 12:6, Mal. 3:10, Heb. 7:1-10)

11. THE GIFTS OF THE SPIRIT. We believe the nine gifts of the Spirit should be manifested in the church today. (I Cor. 12:4-11)

12. THE FRUIT OF THE SPIRIT. We believe the spirit-filled believers will produce the fruit of the spirit in their lives and their walk. (Gal. 5:22,23)

13. THE SECOND COMING OF CHRIST. We believe that Jesus will appear in the clouds for the catching-away of the Bride (Rapture or Blessed Hope) and later return to the earth with His Saints to reign for 1000 years. (Acts 1:11, I Cor. 11:26, Phil. 3:20, I Thess. 4:13-17, Rev. 20:4-6)

14. CHRIST IS THE HEAD. We believe that Christ is the head over all things and that the Church is His Body. (Eph. 1:22-23, Col. 1:18-19)

Article IV.
MEMBERSHIP

4.01 The standard of membership in this church shall be:

1. Evidence of a genuine experience in regeneration (the new birth). (John 1:12-13, 3:3-7, I Peter 1:18-25)

2. Evidence of a consistent Christian life that displays the love of God and obedience to the Gospel of Christ. (Romans 6:4, 13:1, Ephesians 4:17-32, 5:1-2,15, I John 1:6-7)

3. Expression by the person that God has placed him/her in this local church, and that he/she is willing to live by the Tenets of Faith as set forth in this constitution.

4. Faithful support of the church in attendance, in prayer, and in the contribution of tithes and offerings.

5.   Faithful support of the leadership of the church in carrying out the vision and direction of the church as the Holy Spirit leads.

4.02   New member(s) should be recognized and accepted by the Board of Directors and the Elders acting jointly, and the member(s) be introduced as such in any regular service.

4.03   A person may become a member at any age that he/she is able to fulfill the standards for membership set forth in this constitution, but will be eligible to vote after reaching the age of eighteen (18) years.

4.04   Each active member shall have one (1) vote.

4.05   Loss of membership will occur if the standards set forth in this constitution are violated and this loss of membership will be established by the Board of Directors and Elders acting jointly.

Article V.
OFFICES
Board of Directors

5.01   The Board of Directors is defined in the Articles of Incorporation for this church.

1.   A Director shall hold office for the period of 1 (one) year.

2.   A Director can hold innumerable consecutive terms.

Senior Pastor

5.02   The senior pastor is the spiritual and natural head of the local church. He is an elder and as such must meet every qualification for that office as outlined in the Scriptures and recorded in this constitution under the office of elder. (Ephesians 4:11, Hebrews 13:7, 17, I Peter 5:1, I Timothy 3, Titus 1)

1.   His first concern shall be for the spiritual welfare of the church, faithfully preaching and teaching the Word of God and administering the ordinances.

2.   He shall act as the chairman of all church meetings, ex-officio chairman of all auxiliary meetings. No

meeting of any department or office will take place without his presence or approval. The only exception will be a meeting to discuss his removal, and even then he must be given the opportunity to be present for the meeting to be official.

3. The senior pastor shall fulfill his role until his death, until he is led by God to leave that role, or until he has been removed from his office according to the procedure outlined in this constitution.

4. The senior pastor's compensation shall be set by the Board of Directors and the Elders acting jointly. It shall be reviewed annually.

5. If the office of senior pastor is vacated, the Board of Directors and the Elders, acting under the executive guidance of the Presbyters, shall jointly be responsible for supplying ministry to the church for the interim. Under the Presbyters' guidance they shall also be responsible for seeking out a man to fill the senior pastor vacancy. Through prayer and fasting they shall realize that God has called a man to fill that role, and placed within that person the burden to pastor the people. When they have recognized that person, and have accepted the candidate by a two-thirds vote of the Directors and Elders, he shall be presented to the congregation for ratification.

6. The senior pastor may be dismissed from his position only if it is proven that he has ceased to uphold the principle teachings of the church, or that his life has become morally unfit for the ministry, or if it becomes obvious that he is no longer effectively fulfilling his ministerial responsibilities. When the Board of Directors and the Elders are in agreement that this step must be taken, the Board or Presbyters will be contacted by their representative. The Board of Presbyters will act as executives and will call and chair any and all meetings to investigate and act

upon the accusations. Any meeting held without the Presbytery will be deemed unofficial and illegal. The pastor will submit himself to the authority of the Presbytery pending the resolution of all charges. He shall abide by the final decision of the Board of Directors and the Elders, which shall be reached by a two-thirds vote of the total members of these bodies present.

7. The senior pastor shall appoint his assistant pastors, youth leaders, office personnel, education director, teachers, elders, deacons, and other offices needed to administer the spiritual and administrative duties of the church. If any of these offices require remuneration this will necessitate approval by the Directors and Elders acting jointly.

Elders

5.03 The Elders of a local church are responsible for supporting the vision and direction of the church in prayer, fasting, and wise spiritual counsel. They are responsible for spiritual oversight of the membership. An elder must meet the scriptural requirements as outlined in God's Word. (Acts 20:28, Philippians 1:1, I Timothy 3, 5:17, Titus 1, James 5:14)

1. The elders, at the discretion of the senior pastor, will meet as often as necessary to discharge the responsibilities as spiritual leaders of the church body.

2. Elders will act as advisory counsel to the Board of Directors for all spiritual matters of the church. They shall be called by the senior pastor to render such counsel as needed, and in some cases, as set forth in this constitution, joint efforts of the two are mandated.

3. A candidate for elder shall be placed in consideration for eldership by the senior pastor and agreed upon by the elders. He shall then be ordained before

the church body during any service determined by the senior pastor.

4. An elder shall serve the church for as long as he is physically able and spiritually and morally pure. He is to serve under the senior pastor in harmony with his fellow elders.

5. If charges are brought against an elder they shall first be presented to the pastor. If he feels he needs additional counsel to settle the matter, he may bring it before the elders and at his discretion bring in the Board of Presbyters. If the charges are accurate the senior pastor and the elders will determine what disciplinary action will be taken. This decision will be final and binding.

Deacons

5.04 The Deacons in a local church are to support the vision and direction of the church in actions of ministry among the people. They are responsible for the material needs and services of the church. A person who is a deacon shall meet the requirements outlined in Gods Word. (Acts 6:3, I Timothy 3)

1. The deacons, at the discretion of the senior pastor, will meet as often as necessary to discharge their responsibilities.

2. Deacons will serve under direct guidance of the senior pastor and the elders.

3. A candidate for deacon shall be placed in consideration by the senior pastor and agreed upon by the elders. He shall then be ordained before the church body during any service determined by the senior pastor.

4. A deacon shall serve the church for as long as he is physically able and spiritually and morally pure. He is to serve under the senior pastor in harmony with his fellow elders and deacons.

5. If charges are brought against an deacon they shall first be presented to the pastor. If he feels he needs additional counsel to settle the matter, he may bring it before the elders and at his discretion bring in the Board of Presbyters. If the charges are accurate the senior pastor and the elders will determine what disciplinary action will be taken. This decision will be final and binding.

Board of Presbyters

5.05 The leadership of <Corporation name> recognizes that some governmental safeguards are needed, and that it is Biblical to maintain wise counsel. (I Kings 12, Proverbs 11:14, 24:6, Acts 15:6-29) For this reason a Board of Presbyters will be maintained to serve as an advisory and/or arbitrary panel.

1. This Board of Presbyters shall consist of three (3) ordained ministers. These men are to be non-members of <Corporation name>. They shall be appointed by the senior pastor and approved by the Board of Directors and the Elders, and shall be established by the acceptance of a resolution at a regular meeting of these two bodies. Their tenure shall be for an indefinite period.

2. They may be called by the senior pastor or by a representative of the Board of Directors and Elders acting jointly.

3. They shall be called when mandated by this constitution. They may also be called by the pastor to assist in dealing with internal problems or as advisory counsel in such matters as he deems necessary.

4. This board shall have no ecclesiastical authority except on those extreme occasions for which they are called. When they are called, they shall have executive authority and shall work with the pastor, the Board of Directors, and the elders.

Appendix D

SYLLABUS

Since it is my sincere prayer that this material will be used as a teaching reference, I am including a syllabus of the material in this appendix. Feel free to copy and/or modify this syllabus to fit your teaching style and lesson plans. Since I am including the syllabus by chapter, the teacher may have to hand it out in parts to fit the length of classes.

The material is intentionally started on a separate page so that it can be copied and presented without this introduction.

To use it as a teaching aid, you may choose to remove the underlined material, leaving the blank lines to be filled in by those receiving your ministry. The information in the triangle diagram on page 201 and the information in the outlined lists may be left out to be filled in by them as well.

May God richly anoint both you and the material as it is presented.

Leadership and Church Structure

Chapter 1. Scriptural Structure

And Joshua gathered all the tribes of Israel to Shechem, and called for the elders of Israel, and for their heads (some translations say "leaders"), and for their judges, and for their officers; and they presented themselves before God. -Joshua 24:1

And Joshua said unto all the people (Hebrew word implies "attendees")... -Joshua 24:2 a

And Israel served the LORD all the days of Joshua, and all the days of the elders that overlived Joshua, and which had known all the works of the LORD, that he had done for Israel. -Joshua 24:31

I. Proper order. God communicates his message through a <u>leader</u> to <u>others</u> <u>involved</u> <u>in</u> <u>leadership</u> to reach the <u>people</u>.

II. The elements of a proper organization are:

From study text:	From New Testament study:
1. <u>A leader that God chooses</u>	1. <u>Pastor</u>
2. <u>Others in leadership</u>	2. <u>Elders, deasons, teachers, etc.</u>
3. <u>A people that will be lead</u>	3. <u>Congregation</u>

III. Fill in the following structure:

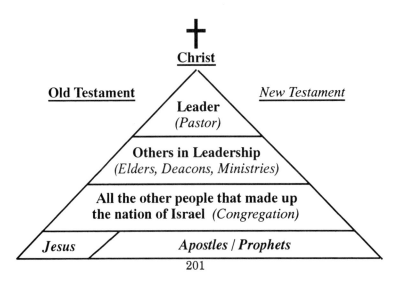

Leadership and Church Structure

Chapter 2. The Leadership Role

For we are labourers together with God: ye are God's husbandry, ye are God's building. According to the grace of God which is given unto me, as a wise masterbuilder, I have laid the foundation, and another buildeth thereon. But let every man take heed how he buildeth thereupon. -I Cor. 3:9, 10

I. The Team.
   A. One of the most important concepts that needs to be developed in any ministry is the leadership <u>team</u>.
   B. <u>Comparing</u> ministries will surely destroy the team concept.

II. Called to Leadership.
   A. It is imperative that there be a God-placed <u>calling</u> in a person's life to the area of leadership he is being placed. *Wherefore the rather, brethren, give diligence to make your [calling and election sure]: for if ye do these things, ye shall never fall. -II Peter 1:10*
   B. God calls us with an <u>holy</u> calling.
   C. Because we are called according to His own <u>purpose</u>, He will never place in our hearts a calling He is not ready and willing to <u>equip</u> us for.
   D. Many times we have to wait on <u>timing</u> and <u>direction</u> after we are called.

III. Setting Leaders into Office.
   A. Pastor.
      1. The person filling the office of pastor must be <u>God placed</u>.
      2. God's design was for the Church to be a <u>theocracy</u>.
   B. Other Leaders.
      1. The <u>pastor</u>, using the counsel of his <u>leaders</u> should appoint people into leadership offices.
      2. The qualifications in God's Word for leadership offices should be used as guidelines when <u>filling</u> the offices and when upholding the <u>integrity</u> of the

offices after they have been filled.

   3. If the Holy Spirit leads you to set in <u>guidelines,</u> He will not lead you to violate them.

IV. Launching Ministries.

   A. List the points found in Paul and Barnabas' ministry in the 13th and 14th chapters of Acts that shows the "cycle" of ministry.

     1. They were called of God to minister.

     2. They ministered to the Lord.

     3. They fasted and prayed while they waited.

     4. They heard the Lord when He spoke direction and timing.

     5. Went out with the backing and support of the people.

     6. They were accountable.

     7. Were willing to start again at point 2, ministering to the Lord.

V. Hindrances to Ministry (Lev. 21:17-20).

   A. List the Old Testament hindrances to the priesthood and the application to ministry today.

1.	<u>Blind man</u>	<u>Has no spiritual vision.</u>
2.	<u>Lame man</u>	<u>Person who is inconvenienced.</u>
3.	<u>Flat nose</u>	<u>Lack of spiritual discernment.</u>
4.	<u>Superfluous</u>	<u>Looking only for gain. Novice.</u>
5.	<u>Broken footed</u>	<u>Impaired spiritual walk.</u>
6.	<u>Broken handed</u>	<u>Can not do.</u>
7.	<u>Crookbacked</u>	<u>Burdened down by things.</u>
8.	<u>Dwarf</u>	<u>Maturity doesn't match spiritual age.</u>
9.	<u>Blemish in the eye</u>	<u>Impaired spiritual sight. Only sees in natural.</u>
10.	<u>Scurvy or scabbed</u>	<u>Son deficiency.</u>
11.	<u>Stones broken</u>	<u>Cannot birth a new Christian.</u>

VI. List the purposes for ministry found in Ephesians 4:11-14.
  1. For the equipping (perfecting) of the saints.
  2. For the work of the ministry.
  3. For the edification of the body of Christ.
  4. For unity.
  5. For maturity (a perfect man).
  6. To allow the fullness of Christ in us and the Church.
  7. For solidness.

VII. List seven principles of leadership.
  1. A leader must carry responsibilities.
  2. A leader needs teaching.
  3. A leader needs backing and covering.
  4. A leader must meet the qualifications of office.
  5. A leader must demonstrate the proper characteristics of a leader.
  6. A leader must have a proper attitude.
  7. A leader must retain integrity.

VIII. List seven characteristics of a leader.
  1. A man who loves God.
  2. A man who trusts God.
  3. A man who has experienced God's ways.
  4. A man who leads by hearing God.
  5. A man who shoulders responsibility.
  6. A man who can be an example.
  7. A man with a compassionate heart.

IX. Interactions of Leaders.
  A. One of the greatest responsibilities of a leader is for him to place other ministries, delegate their responsibilities, instruct them in how to carry out these responsibilities, and then encourage them as they do.
  B. A leader's responsibility to those under his care include:
  1. Recognize them.
  2. Honour and promote them.
  3. Support them.
  4. Correct them.

C. A work limited to one person will never grow beyond that person's <u>capabilities</u>.

D. Just as the pastor is the example of leadership, each leader must be the example of how to <u>operate</u> under that leadership.

E. You cannot be a leader is you don't know how to <u>submit</u>.

F. We can support our pastor (or other leader) with <u>prayer</u> support, our <u>voice</u> of approval, and our <u>action</u> support.

X. Priorities and Relationships.

A. We must develop our relationships in the following priority:

1. Me to God.
2. Me to Me.
3. Me to Spouse.
4. Me to Children.
5. Me to my Job.
6. Me to my Ministry.
7. Me to Others.

Leadership and Church Structure

Chapter 3. The Pastor

And I will give you pastors according to mine heart, which shall feed you with knowledge and understanding. -Jer. 3:15

I.   A pastor is a leader who has been <u>called</u> and <u>placed</u> by God to <u>shepherd</u> those people placed under his care.

II.   A pastor is an <u>elder</u> and as such must meet all the qualifications for that office.

III.   We find no particular scripture in the Bible declaring to set a pastor into office, yet we see a <u>pattern</u> clearly visible in both <u>Jesus' ministry</u> and in the <u>New Testament</u> Church.

IV.   A pastor has God given <u>authority</u> in the local church.

V.   A pastor must also be God's <u>mouthpiece</u> to the people.

VI.   Because God respects the principles in His Word, including "chain of command," the pastor will receive direction from God <u>ahead</u> of those given to the people.

VII.   God will speak to others in the church, but He will never <u>contradict</u> what He has spoken to the pastor.

VIII.   A pastor needs <u>promotion</u> and will receive it from his <u>pastor</u>, from his <u>leadership</u>, and from the <u>congregation</u>.

Leadership and Church Structure

Chapter 4. Other Leadership Ministries

I.   Organized leadership, overseen by the leader (pastor), will work together to carry out the ministry of governments in the local church.

II. This leadership team is made up of elders, deacons, and other supportive ministries.

III. Elders.

    A. Elders are appointed to the local body to oversee the carrying out of its vision and direction through prayer and fasting, through teaching ministries, and through the giving of counsel.

    B. List the scriptural qualifications for the office of elder.

1. Blameless.
2. Husband of one wife.
3. Vigilant.
4. Sober.
5. Of good behavior.
6. Hospitable.
7. Apt to teach.
8. Not given to wine.
9. No striker.
10. Not greedy of filthy lucre.
11. Patient.
12. Not a brawler.
13. Not Covetous.
14. One that can rule well his own house.
15. Not a novice.
16. Good report with those outside the church.
17. Holy.
18. Steward of God.
19. Not self-willed.
20. Not soon angry.
21. Lover of good men.
22. Just.
23. Temperate.
24. Holding fast to the faithful Word.

    C. The elders are commissioned to oversee the matters of the local church administering to any spiritual needs that arise. *Let the elders that rule well be counted worthy of double honour, especially they who labour in the word and doctrine. -I Tim. 5:17*

IV. Deacons.
   A. Deacons are appointed to the local body to support its vision and direction with actions of <u>ministering among</u> the people.
   B. The list of qualifications for a deacon include five of which were already given to the elders:
      1. Not given to much wine.
      2. Not greedy of filthy lucre.
      3. Blameless.
      4. Husband of one wife.
      5. One that can rule well his own household.
   C. The list also include three added qualifications:
      1. Not doubletongued.
      2. Holding the mystery of the faith in pure conscience.
      3. Wives that meet standards.
   D. Deacons primarily administer to any <u>physical</u> needs that might acquire the attention of the church.
      For they that have used the office of a deacon well purchase to themselves a good degree, and great boldness of faith which is in Christ Jesus. -I Tim 3:13
V. Other Supportive Ministries.
   A. All supportive ministries should meet the criteria for <u>membership</u> and for <u>leadership</u>.
   B. Supportive ministries may fall under the area of <u>fivefold ministry</u> or under <u>supportive gifts</u> (Eph. 4:11, Rom. 12:6-8).
   C. Some supportive gifts may serve under the role of <u>governments</u> (I Cor. 12:28).

Leadership and Church Structure

Chapter 5. The Congregation

I.   The congregation can be defined as a people who can gather in <u>unity</u> and in <u>support</u> of their local body and their leadership.

II.   It is imperative that everyone know that God has <u>placed</u> them where they are in the body of Christ.

And I (Jesus) say also unto thee, That thou art Peter, and upon this Rock I will build my church; and the gates of hell shall not prevail against it. -Mat. 16:18

Ye also, [as lively stones], are built up a spiritual house, and holy priesthood, to offer up spiritual sacrifices, acceptable to God by Jesus Christ. -I Peter 2:5

III.   There are four characteristics of a strong congregation.
1. A united people.
2. A people with an ear.
3. A supportive people.
4. A people of prayer.

IV.   List the four areas of a Christian's prayer life.
1. Supplications.
2. Prayers.
3. Intercessions.
4. Thanksgiving.

V.   Every believer is called to the ministry of <u>reconciliation</u>.

VI.   Many will be involved in the ministry of <u>helps</u>.

VII.   A pastor has responsibilities to the congregation. He is to <u>teach</u> and <u>nurture</u> them, <u>correct</u> them, and to <u>involve</u> them.

Not forsaking the assembling of ourselves together, as the manner of some is; but exhorting one another: and so much more, as ye see the day approaching. -Heb. 10:25

Leadership and Church Structure

Chapter 6. Governmental Structure

And the Lord answered me, and said, Write the vision, and make it plain upon tables, that he may run that readeth it. –Hab. 2:2

I.   When a ministry becomes incorporated, certain <u>legal</u> requirements will be imposed that will effect the <u>structure</u>.

II.   There are two reasons why a church may display different structure:

    1.   The structure that works for one may not support the vision and direction of another.

    2.   Sometimes church structure is inherited.

III. To become incorporated, the church must file a copy of its <u>Articles</u> of <u>Incorporation</u> with the state.

IV.   A document that allows a corporation to further define its offices, operations, and procedures is the <u>Constitution</u> or the <u>By-Laws</u>.

V.   If changes are not defined in the organization's documents, it will have to operate under the <u>defaults</u> of the state.

VI.   An organization may choose to have one or more <u>Policy</u> <u>and</u> <u>Procedures</u> <u>Manual</u> to define in greater detail the operations of specific areas.

VII. An organization will have a <u>Board</u> <u>of</u> <u>Directors</u> that will elect <u>officers</u> to carry out the administrative duties.

VIII. A <u>registered</u> <u>agent</u> is that person(s) reported to the state as the contact person for the corporation.

IX.   An <u>agent</u> is that person(s) who is empowered by the board of directors to have authority to perform duties in the management of the property and affairs of the corporation.

X.   It is advisable for an organization to have available <u>advisory</u> <u>council(s)</u>.

XI.   Churches automatically have <u>tax</u> exemption with the IRS, but may need to check with the <u>state</u> for other exemptions.

About this book ...

Reading through the manuscript, it is clear that Dennis Moses has a clear understanding of Christian leadership. Not only does he write on the subject of leadership, but has also set the example of leadership in many areas within the local church. He's not writing from theory only, but more from the practical standpoint.

Dr. John Bosman
International Speaker and Author
President and Founder of JWB Institute
for Dynamic Church Leadership
Pastor, Glad Tidings Assembly of God
Lake Charles, Louisiana

In the Church of Jesus Christ, perhaps no issue is as crucial as leadership and how each leader is to function in ministry. Dennis Moses has written a book that addresses the issue head-on from a biblical yet practical perspective.

It has been my privilege and pleasure to fellowship with Dennis on occasion. Each time I have been impressed with his sincere and humble attitude about spiritual things. His keen insights about leadership and church government, and his ability to pass on this knowledge is a blessing to the Body of Christ.

I feel certain that the chapters in this volume will do much in clarifying and informing the reader on how to escape some of the mistakes and pitfalls which have led to division in local churches and havoc in ministry.

David Cook
President
International Bible College
San Antonio, Texas

Dennis has done an excellent job of dealing with the subject of leadership and church government from a solid Biblical standpoint. He has served Abundant Life Church as co-pastor and associate pastor faithfully for ten years. During this time he was interim pastor at a neighboring church for three months. While interim he helped the church locate and set in the present pastor. He also served this church, which was previously his home church, and another nearby church as interim before coming on staff with us. This book is the fruit of his ministry and result of multiple hours of research.

I have known Dennis for many years. Ministering to those in church leadership has been a burden of his heart for several years. The Lord has used him to give solid counsel in this area. He is an excellent minister of the Word. He has shown an ability to lead during difficult times.

Robert A. "Bob" Rutherford (my pastor)
Pastor
Abundant Life Church of DeRidder
DeRidder, Louisiana

It has been my pleasure to witness the unfolding of these principles from a two-part series that Dennis shared in the church we previously pastored in Texas to its present form. This is a book that every leader and everyone who loves their leaders should heed to and study.

Dub Williams
Missionary Statesman
Christian Educator
Pastor
Marshall Assembly of God
Marshall, Minnesota

Many times we hear people say, "I wish someone would write a book to help pastors of churches." Well, Dennis has done it. I especially appreciated the down–to–earth way he has blended theory with practical experience. I believe this material is written in a fashion that will be easily understood even by the most inexperienced administrator. Sometimes we get bogged down in what is "politically correct" and lose sight of "what works." Thank you Dennis for taking the time to do this work. My prayer is that many ministers needing such information as you have dealt with here will avail themselves of it. Take time to read the material offered here. Use what will help you. Never try to copy any material to the letter but mold it to you individual needs. I do not doubt that you will be benefited by this book.

Dr. Harold G. Eiland
Pastor
Christian Fellowship Church
Cutoff, Louisiana

To everything there is something that is identified as the supporting framework. To the human body, the skeletal system is that supporting framework. Without it the body would be a useless pile of muscle and potential. The body of Christ is no different; it also requires a supporting framework. This book gives great light into God's ordained framework for the local body. I would recommend its reading to anyone interested in developing a strong framework for their local body.

E. J. Dantin
Pastor
Leesville Full Gospel Church
Leesville, Louisiana
